WHEN DEATH SPEAKS

Listen, Learn, and Love

Stephen Lloyd Garrett

John,

RRRRR

♡ Stephen

Copyright © 2013 by Stephen Lloyd Garrett

First Edition – June 2013

ISBN

978-1-4602-1625-5 (Hardcover)
978-1-4602-1626-2 (Paperback)
978-1-4602-1627-9 (eBook)

Produced by:

FriesenPress

Suite 300 – 852 Fort Street
Victoria, BC, Canada V8W 1H8

www.friesenpress.com

Distributed to the trade by The Ingram Book Company

TABLE OF CONTENTS

DEDICATION

This book is written for you all and dedicated to five amazing, courageous, loving, radiant, inspiring, crazy women.

Sonora Grace Wallace—my wife and inspiration

Diane Wallace—my mother-in-law and editor

Marjorie Garrett—my mother

The late Jody Garrett—my sister

Barbara Cameron—my photographer

Stephen

Every issue, challenge, situation or conflict is always and opportunity to practice the art of loving even more. —Stephen L. Garrett

TO CHANGE THE WAY YOU LOOK AT DEATH REQUIRES A LEAP OF FAITH

WHY THIS BOOK?

To change the Conversation about death from denial and fear to acceptance and inspiration.

This book is about my own personal adventures in changing my approach to death from one of denial and fear to one of acceptance and inspiration. I hope that by walking with me along my path you will gain some insights and understanding of how you too can alter your own approach to death. My wish for each reader is that you would have a much richer appreciation for all the details of taking care of a loved one before, during, and after death, as well as cultivating a new approach to dying that is more open, embracing, and loving, while equipping you with new tools to deal with it all.

I was in Bali in September 2010. It was a grand adventure; I experienced two truly amazing weeks that were full of surprises, new insights, and a deepening of personal understanding. The journey included all manner of wonderful events and happenings, from driving a motorcycle on the narrow city streets of Ubud in rush hour, to enjoying some wonderful food, song, and dance. We toured amazing temples, met with exceptional teachers and healers, and took part in one of the most breathtaking and lavish ceremonies I have ever witnessed.

The ceremony was a cremation for a member of the Bali Royal Family. When I got to the site, I couldn't tell if it was a joyful, celebratory parade, or if it was a cremation. It sure felt like the former! The cremation ceremony was so public, so joyful, so real, and so loving that it bowled me over.

The disparity between this Balinese cremation and our North American approach to the end of life was shocking! The stark contrast caused me to recognize how much we are in denial of death within much of our North American culture. This sense of shock inspired me to write this book and do my best to help change the way we look at death here in my home country of Canada.

A BIT OF BACKGROUND

I have spent some time in my life as a hospice volunteer and as a hospice coordinator, and am currently involved in the funeral business as a cremationist. I have first-hand experience of how we 'manage' death here in Canada. I have also faced my own share of death in my own family and circle of friends. I recently read Senator Carstair's report on hospice and palliative care in Canada entitled *Raising the Bar,* and was startled to see in clear print what is happening in dealing with such a natural and fundamental part of life. Although we have made strides forward in caring for the dying, we have a long way yet to go.

Do you know the majority of people in our country, between 70 to 80 percent, are not being served at all when it comes to living, growing, and evolving through death? Do you know that we spend more healthcare dollars during the final weeks and months before death than we do in our entire lives?

I know that we have made strides in this field over the years and yet I wonder:

- *How do we teach our people to look at death, to talk about it openly, to treat it as a natural aspect of life?*
- *How do we prepare our families and communities to be much more self-reliant in this intimate and important time of their lives?*
- *How do we support the ones dying in a way that honors and celebrates the life lived, as opposed to just mourning the loss of a loved one?*
- *How do we talk about creating a wonderful end-of-life celebration that the dying desire and deserve?*
- *How do we turn an archenemy such as death—something we are conditioned to avoid at all costs—into an inspiring teacher and ally?*

These questions need to be answered, as we will soon be experiencing a wave of death that has never before been witnessed. This wave, of course, is the result of the natural passing of the baby-boomer generation. From my perspective as an active hospice volunteer and cremationist, I recognize the urgency to not only prepare the staff and volunteers of societies, agencies, and corporations, but also family and community members.

The real help will be found in providing tools, skills, techniques, training, and building the capacity of our families and communities in order that they become much more self reliant and response-able for the intimate event we call death.

It is a way of handing back to people the skills we have professionalized over the decades, as well as reversing the steps we have taken as individuals to avoid the reality of dealing with death. These steps have, in fact, denied death instead of accepting it as a natural and necessary part of life. These are steps that have led us right to the doors of local hospices and palliative care services. We need to move forward now and prepare ourselves to deal with death in new, open, and exciting ways—ways that will create an environment rich in the celebration of a life well-lived, of relationships fulfilled, and of wisdom passed along.

In saying all this, I also want to acknowledge all the amazing progress made over the years and give huge credit to all the people—professionals, volunteers, and other individuals—who have dedicated their time, energy, passion, and heart to caring for the dying. It is on your very shoulders that the new ways, new structures, and new approaches will stand. Thank you!

I am on a mission to bring even more openness and discussion to the topic of death, and to shine some light on a topic that many of us ponder only in the privacy of our own minds. I intend to change the conversations we have about dying, taking it from fear and denial to acceptance and inspiration—to turn the Grim Reaper into an inspiring teacher. Read on, my friends!

Live as if you were to die tomorrow.
Learn as if you were to live forever. —Mahatma Gandhi

CHAPTER ONE

Death, The Taboo Topic – How We Got Here

Death is not the greatest loss in life.
The greatest loss is what dies inside us while we live.—Norman Cousins

---

IN THE BEGINNING

When I was a young boy, I spent many a summer on the family farm. I shoveled all kinds of manure, did all manner of chores in the barn and around the farm, learned lots, ate a ton of great farm-fresh food, and slept really well!

One of the things I remember is that death was not a big deal. An animal would die or be slaughtered for food, and life simply went on. Death wasn't spoken of, nor was it hidden away—it just *was*. Death happened, and life always carried on as before. It was taken in stride as a normal part of life. Now, of course, these deaths were that of animals, not family members, yet the example really made an impression on me.

These experiences of death were healthy ones, and as a result, I accepted death as a natural and normal part of life. My questions about death were answered lovingly and with honesty. There was nothing left for me to be anxious or frightened about. Death on the farm was no big deal; it had its place in the natural order of farm life.

As a result, I had no fear of death. It was just *with* me.

THE DENIAL TRAINING BEGINS

Many years later I experienced, firsthand, the death of Grandpa Joe. I was twelve years old. It was 1961.

Grandpa Joe's death was very different than my initial experiences with death on the farm. So different, in fact, that it really confused me. I remember a lot of scurrying around, lots of emotions, lots of sadness, and many long faces. I also remember being in the funeral home with many adults around, and most of us kids were outside not knowing quite what to do. The whole scene seemed weird to me.

Grandpa Joe was lying in a brown wood box. He was dressed in a business suit. His eyes were closed. He looked really white. His body was stiff and cold when I touched his face and hands. I got into trouble for doing that, which confused me even more. People would go up to this box and do something or say something. I couldn't hear or understand them because their backs were to me. An adult told me it was a private matter and not to ask again about what was going on.

But I had lots of questions! I couldn't find anyone who would answer them. Everyone seemed so busy and preoccupied or just unwilling to talk with me about death.

Why is Grandpa's skin so white? Why are some people crying so much? What is he in the box for? Why is he dressed in a suit? Where is he going? Why does he have makeup on? Why does he feel so cold? Where do dead people go? Will he be lonely? Will he miss me? When am I going to die?

I couldn't find any answers, so I started to make things up in my own mind, creating my own answers based on fear and uncertainty, based on the reactions I saw in the adults around me. It felt like there was something wrong with death, and that it was somehow bad.

That night I had some dreams that really scared me! I dreamt of my own death. This dream of dying kept me awake night after night and week after week. I was puzzled and scared, and felt I had no one to go to with my questions. I didn't want to bother anybody with my bad dreams as they were all about death, and no one seemed to want to talk about it.

A few days after the funeral, no one seemed to be talking about it; everyone seemed to have put Grandpa's death behind them and were carrying on with their lives. I learned to be afraid of death and to keep it private. I thought I had to do it all alone.

Deeply lodged in my mind and body was the ever-present haunting memory of death. Unconsciously I was creating a library of snap shots that contained facets of my experience of Grandpa Joe's death that became unfinished business for me. I felt others didn't understand me or the suppressed emotions I kept inside. I didn't understand the things other people said and did around this loss.

Finally, and with much relief, it all seemed to vanish as my life as a young boy again took over. Time passed and memories of Grandpa Joe's death faded into the darker realms of my mind, not to be accessed or spoken of again by me or anyone else for that matter. It seemed like it was something that I was not to bring up or talk about, so I didn't!

The fear of death seems to be the biggest deterrent of all, likely because it can be so hard to get straight answers to questions about death when we are younger. Here are some common fears many of us experience from time to time that arise mostly out of ignorance. We pass them on to others through the indirect yet observable ways we deal with the inevitability of death.

See if you recognize some of your own here:

Fear of pain and suffering: Many people are afraid that they will meet death with excruciating pain and suffering. This is common in many healthy people, and of course, it is often felt by patients dying of potentially painful diseases.

Fear of the unknown: Death is the ultimate unknown. No one has survived to tell us what happens afterward. It's in our human nature to want to understand and make sense of the world around us, but death can never be fully understood while we are still alive.

Fear of non-existence: Many people fear that they will cease existing after death. This fear isn't confined only to the non-religious or atheists. Many people of faith worry that their belief in an afterlife won't be real after all.

Fear of eternal punishment: Again, this belief isn't only for the most spiritually devout. People from every religious sect, and even those with no religion at all, may fear that they will be punished for what they did—or did *not* do—here on Earth.

Fear of loss of control: Our human nature seeks control over situations. Death is out of our realm of control. This is very scary for most of us. Some will even attempt to hold death at bay with excessively careful behavior and rigorous health checks.

Fear of what will become of loved ones: Probably the most common fear of death among new parents, single parents, and caregivers is the fear of what will happen to those entrusted to our care if we die.

THE DENIAL WALL GOES UP

Years later, I got to go through it all over again, this time as an adult. All the questions I had about Grandpa Joe's death, all the fear I stuffed down, all the anger I felt yet held back, and the roller-coaster ride of emotions all came roaring back as I got the news that my younger sister Jody had died suddenly and unexpectedly.

It was Friday May 5th, 1988, at about 10:00 pm. As I opened the door to my second-floor brownstone apartment in downtown Toronto, I heard my telephone ringing off the hook. It had the ring of urgency; I didn't want to answer it, and yet I was compelled.

It was my brother-in-law, Roy. He couldn't really speak; all he was able to utter was, "Jody is gone." and he quickly passed the telephone to his Mom. As she spoke to me, the story began to unfold. It all seemed like some sort of otherworldly happening. I heard the words… *Jody died today*. She was helping some friends move, and felt a little tired after the move, so she lay down on the couch for a nap. An hour or so later, her friends tried to wake her for dinner and they were unable to. She had died in her sleep.

I heard all the words, and I understood them, but on some level I was unable to let the reality of Jody's death in. On my drive up to my parent's home to give them the news of their daughter's death, I felt as if I was in some kind of twilight zone, almost like I was outside of my own life.

As I spoke with my Mom and Dad about Jody's passing, I felt like some kind of automaton. I was getting the information across to my folks, but I was lost in space somewhere, not really present, though it looked like I was. Looking back at it now, I realize that what was happening was that Jody's demise put me back in touch with the experience of Grandpa Joe's passing which was still stored in my mind and body. All the stuff I didn't complete and all the questions I didn't get answered back then were all wrapped around this new and current loss. I actually felt like a little boy who was totally afraid of death again!

I travelled with my family from Toronto to Ste. Catherine's, Ontario, where Jody had lived with her husband Roy. We did all the regular stuff around funerals—the planning, funeral home, church, obituary and calls to friends and family. I was doing my share of all this from that same surreal place, that detached and almost indifferent place. Though I was acting like I accepted the reality of Jody's death, I most certainly had not let into my reality the *fact* that she was dead. I was simply going through the motions.

The funeral home, the throngs of people, the full parking lot at the church, the sermon, and the procession all went off as planned. It was a wonderful day, and the love of friends and family was palpable. Yet still I seemed to be some-where else. I was lost and not really present as to what was really going on for me emotionally. It didn't hit me until I was lowering the casket that held Jody into the ground. Boom! It was like a bomb going off! My sister was dead.

All the emotions I had not been really present to came rushing up all in one moment. I was overwhelmed and could barely contain myself. Yet, in that moment, all I could do was muster but one tear. I choked back the rest for a later time and got on with the rest of the day.

Several weeks later I did my best to get on with the rest of my life, doing all I could to put Jody's death behind me. And so I went on not really dealing with Jody's death at all.

I again unconsciously continued to add even more to my collection of snapshots about death. I tucked even more thoughts, emotions, and misunder-standings into my growing library of the fear of death.

This can be the way it goes for many of us. We simply stack up all these incomplete emotions and thoughts, and store them away to fester and gnaw at us whenever death shows up, or whenever memories arise unexpectedly.

© 2010 barbara cameron pix

WE TEND TO DEAL WITH DEATH ALL ALONE. WE ARE AFRAID TO TALK ABOUT IT

DEATH—MY OBSERVATIONS OVER THE YEARS

I have watched people dying and witnessed what goes on around death, learned about how we handle it, and what we do to try and make it go away. Even though there are great people working to open up the box we have built around death, they are fighting against big odds: the system. When you look at life going on around you, you will see the fear and denial. You will see what many of us do to avoid this reality, and even in some cases how people profit from the collective fear of death, consciously or unconsciously. Here is what I see about death and dying from the perspective of a North American:

FIGHTING DEATH IS GREAT FOR THE ECONOMY.

Watch television and you will see exactly what I mean by this. How much money is generated by the whole face-lift, Botox, stay young-looking industry? Close to one billion dollars annually in Canada! The war against life-threatening diseases like cancer, efforts to build bigger biceps through steroids, chemical cures for erectile dysfunction, and the eradication of child-birth stretch marks are some examples of our quest for the fountain of youth. Keeping patients alive for as long as possible at great expense and profit is another example, as is the drug companies' pain-free focus, and our demand for it.

Our dark, sensationalized approach to death is obvious. Check out all the television shows which feature an unreal fascination with death—all of the shows and computer games with warriors and weapons and someone having to suffer or die. Isn't all this activity actually desensitizing and death-denying?

All this activity speaks clearly to me:

- Fight death at all costs.
- Create hope; rational or not.
- Make it better.
- Make it go away.

DEATH IS A BIG DEAL—IT ENDS PHYSICAL LIFE.

Death ends life, takes our loved ones away, and can cause great pain and suffering. The Grim Reaper is always lurking in the background. Death can be seen like a big stop sign.

DEATH MEANS I GET LEFT BEHIND.

On some level, we all have an innate feeling that it is us who are being left behind. It is not so much a thought as it is subtle intuition. So in fact, we are mourning our own sense of being left abandoned or alone, and of course, not liking this feeling, we deny it too!

DEATH IS THE UNKNOWN, AND MANY OF US HAVE LEARNED TO FEAR IT.

Oftentimes in our culture we are taught to fear the unknown. What is around the corner? What will happen *if*? This approach to the unknown by most of us engenders fear and a sense of holding back. Death is the great unknown and ought to be feared.

DEATH IS THE ENEMY.

Death comes to all of us at any age, any gender, any race, and any demographic. It seems to make sense when it comes naturally to older folks. Yet death comes to all ages. Is it fair that a two-year-old dies, that a daughter predeceases a father, or that a young man gets killed by a drunk driver? No, it doesn't seem fair, and this sense of injustice can and does turn death into an enemy.

DON'T THINK ABOUT DEATH AND FOR GOD'S SAKE DON'T TALK ABOUT IT.

Don't think about, hell, don't *talk* about it! When we speak of death, it makes it real, and we are doing our best to avoid it, so we best not talk of death at all, even when it is present in the room. Let's instead talk about hope and everything will be OK.

Death is a topic that is almost impolite to talk about. If you do, make sure the one dying is out of earshot. More importantly, speak in vague and obscure terms that do not mention the "D" word at all!

DEATH IS A COIN TOSS.

I am either going to heaven or hell, and there's either life after death, or there's nothing. What a nasty set of options. I'd rather not face it if those are my only alternatives.

So we create this image or energy around death from all these ideas we have about it. The seeds of these ideas of death grow and expand as we move along through our lives. Even though they are based on assumption and fear, the thoughts take shape and really block our ability to live with death in a manner that is based on authenticity, reality, compassion, and love. Here is a list of the beliefs that got in my way for some time:

- Death is the big limiter—it ends life
- Death is the unknown, and because of that, should be feared
- Death is not fair
- Don't think about death
- Death is a coin toss
- For God's sake, don't talk about it

Then add to this list of beliefs our fear of the following:

- Fear of pain and suffering
- Fear of the unknown
- Fear of non-existence
- Fear of eternal punishment
- Fear of loss of control
- Fear of what will become of loved ones

Create your own list and add it to mine if you wish, and you will start to see why death can appear so daunting.

Check it out for yourself, my friends. Go and visit several places where death is present, such as the waiting room on the cardiac care ward or cancer wing of a hospital. Stop by a funeral parlor and see how artificial everything can be. Be open to what is really going on, and you will begin to feel the suppression and denial of death that I am talking about.

Are the people you are encountering open, free in expression, and genuinely loving in what they are doing as they go about their day? Or rather are they walled off, professionally distant, and business-like? Are they protecting themselves from the real feelings and emotions that are in that space?

We are a society that denies and fights against death.

We are far from embracing it or even accepting it as an opening or opportunity from which we can grow. We tend to neglect the people that are close to the one that passed on. They are deeply and profoundly affected by the death over a long period of time— oftentimes negatively—which affects the quality of their own life.

LEAPING FORWARD IN TIME TO A DIFFERENT APPROACH TO DEATH'S DOORWAY.

I'm going to tell you a story about my Dad's death. It was a challenging yet glorious time! This may sound odd to you, but for me it was a wonderful celebration of my father's life, and a really healthy way to say goodbye to a loved one.

This story illustrates a contrast to how we usually handle death and was an experience that confronted my own fear and uncertainty. All the things I assumed while growing up in a death-denying culture I was subsequently able to set aside. I will explain how I was able to make this leap of faith from denial to acceptance as we go through the later chapters of this book. But for now, please enjoy the tale of Lloyd's death:

Dad had been under the weather for some time and wasn't doing well at all (North American-speak for Lloyd was dying). Over the previous several years, his eyesight and hearing had started to go, too! He had lived a full life, and his body was confirming this truth in the later years of his life.

He had been in the hospital for several weeks, and his health was poor and getting much worse. The medical team had him plugged into all kinds of machines. Tubes were stuck in every possible orifice. The staff team was all doing their best to keep Dad alive.

The telephone rang one day—it was Dad. I remember it well. The ring had that familiar sound of importance. He said that he needed to talk with me, his eldest son. I had the sense, as he had never before made this kind of request, that things were not going too well. I was right.

"Son," Dad spoke, "This whole hospital thing, all the machines and tubes, all the drugs— this is not loving-kindness."

"Tell me some more, Dad," I replied

"Well, son, I can't do anything but lie here. I can't golf, play crib, or enjoy television. My friends can only stay for short visits. I can't move much. This isn't the way I want to go out," Dad relayed. "Besides everyone in this damn place is dying!"

"I get it, Dad—it must be awful there trapped in a hospital bed when all you really want to do is be with friends, golf, and enjoy life as you always did," was my response.

There was a long seemingly endless pause. Then he said, "I need to make some changes and a big decision. Can you help me?"

I knew what was coming. Dad had always been a vital fellow and lived life fully. Being trapped in a hospital bed and strapped in by tubes and machines was not in Dad's frame of reference. He couldn't stand it, and I must say I really understood him; in that moment, I really felt him deeply.

"So, Dad, what is it you need to do?" I asked, already knowing the answer.

"Son, I want to have the doctors unplug me and take me off all these damn machines. I will live as long as my body keeps me alive. I would rather that than being kept in this living hell."

"Dad, I love you and I really get what you need. I support you fully, so go ahead, call Mom and your doctors, and have them unplug your from all that life support stuff," I said bravely. I was crying as I knew that this would likely be the last time I would ever talk to my father again.

"You are doing the right thing, Dad," I continued. "Trust your heart as I do—call your wife and children and then let go. You have had a great life—man, what a blast you have had! I am so proud of how you have lived and loved." I said full of love and pride for my Dad. "I understand Dad, it's OK. Go ahead if it feels like it is your time to go."

"Thanks Stephen, I'm so glad I called. And thanks for loving me all these years through our good times and our bad times. You are a fine son," Dad said with love.

"I love you too Dad!"

We chatted a bit more about sports and little stuff, told some silly jokes and then said good-bye, both of us knowing it would be the very last time we would talk. The work had been done. Father and son had lovingly and magically completed and fulfilled their relationship, both knowing that the love between them was mutual and complete. Wow!

That was the last time I ever spoke with my Dad. He did what he needed to do and was dead later that night. He died knowing that he was well-loved by his eldest son. I let my Dad go in love knowing that he had always done his best.

I cried when Mom called to let me know that he had died, more from joy than from loss: Joy because I knew that Dad and I were complete, and that there was nothing left to say. All that remained was the love to feel and remember.

I flew to Toronto from Vancouver two days later, and my, did we create a joyful celebration of Dad's life.

We set up a wonderful gathering for Lloyd, and for all the extended family and friends who would join us. We planned to have fun, enjoy each other's company, and we shared fond memories. We hauled pictures out, memorabilia, and all sorts of stuff that reminded all of us about Dad's well-lived life.

We set up displays at the funeral home and also in the church. We organized how we all could speak and what the theme of the days would be. We had fun with family and friends and truly enjoyed telling Dad's really bad jokes, drinking a little whisky in Lloyd's honor, and just being together while remembering highlights of his life. It was just how Dad would have wanted it. I know he enjoyed it too! It was a wonderful celebration of a life complete!

So what really happened and how was I able to move from denying death to embracing it?

I do not fear death. I had been dead for billions and billions of years before I was born, and had not suffered the slightest inconvenience from it.—Mark Twain

CHAPTER TWO

Shifting from Denial to Embrace—Changing the Lenses

Once you accept your own death, all of a sudden you're free to live. You no longer care about your reputation. You no longer care except so far as your life can be used tactically to promote a cause you believe in.—Saul Alinsky

So what happened? How was I able to go from being a kid who was totally scared of death, *frightened to death of it*, to become an adult that was fully open, loving, and willing to face his father's death head-on with total compassion? What did I learn, how did I change, what did I do?

Well, I'd love to tell you. It was and still is quite an adventure. Are you ready for the story—at least the highlights of it? Great. Let's flash back and see how it all evolved!

After my sister Jody died back in May of 1988 I went into a depression. Some call it survivor's guilt. I was having a heck of a time dealing with all my emotions—anger, guilt, fear, sadness and oddly, a feeling of gratitude. It was a complicated puzzle, at least in my own mind.

I was having trouble sleeping, was having a tough time focusing at work, struggled socially, and had a hard time on the squash court. I was almost totally consumed by thoughts and feelings surrounding the death of Jody. It was bringing up all kinds of memories and future worries.

It was as if I were going crazy. I hid it well, but those close to me were a little worried about my state of mind.

I was having lunch with Keith, a friend of mine, and just happened to mention a tiny bit of what was going on for me. He gave me the name and number of a woman he was certain could help me through this time of adjustment. I stuffed the number in my suit pocket and offered a muffled thank you. I quickly changed the subject, and we went on with the meal and had a less intense conversation. We finished a cup of coffee and we both headed back to our respective offices.

By the time I got home that evening I had totally forgotten about my chat with Keith. It was only as I was getting changed that I stumbled across the card he gave me. So I placed her card by my telephone at home with a weak intention to call her someday.

The days went by and I never made the call. I was too afraid to look inside, and too embarrassed to ask for help. All the while, though, the internal pressure of thoughts, emotions, questions, and concerns continued to build. The weeks turned into a couple of months. I still couldn't bring myself to make the call.

One day I just couldn't stand the emotional pressure any more, nor, for that matter, my pathetic procrastination. I resolved to call this woman. Yet each day when I came home I would pick up the telephone, dial the number, and hang up just before it rang. I was afraid to ask for help and support and felt like such a failure. I felt so weak, as if I were a lost little boy.

One Friday night I was so distraught that I could no longer stop myself. Picking up the telephone—and actually calling this time—I stayed on the line and spoke with her. We set up some dates to meet and do 'sessions'. As I hung up the telephone I had a strange sense of relief. I had actually taken a small step to get some help with the grief I was carrying.

I slept well that night.

I spent a couple of months with this wonderful therapist and felt tremendously helped by her, making progress in dealing with and understanding my emotions. I got clear regarding what the grief process was for me and how to continue to move forward, and with her support, I was able to fully complete the grief process I was going through regarding Jody's death. At the end of our sessions I felt satisfied and at peace with it all.

I learned something:

The grief and loss journey does require guidance and mentoring from someone who has walked the path just ahead of you.

As a side benefit of my grief and loss work, I met a new community of people, a group of folks who loved life and were doing their best to live a life based on good-hearted principles. I was very inspired by what they were up to and jumped into the community with both feet.

Though having spent the better part of my life in the world of banking and investment finance, my deeper heart had always longed for a spiritual path. I continued to work in the investment business to support myself and my family while spending almost all of my free time studying, practicing new ways of spiritual living, and volunteering with this new group of people.

The result of my reawakened spiritual life was a recognition that the way I was making a living had to soon come to an end. My heart was no longer in it and I was being drawn headlong into a life of social work—a life of serving others.

Eleven months later I left my life as I had lived it for twenty-three years. Though my family and friends were sad to see my wife and I leave, they supported me fully as they knew I was following my heart.

Now living on the west coast of British Columbia, my life of service had begun. Once we settled into our rural lifestyle, I started casting about to find some employment in the social services field. Find it I did. There were several part-time jobs: one as a youth worker, another as a senior's support worker, and another as a hospice coordinator. There were different jobs in between all in the helping professions of health care, addictions, and youth worker. All supported my growth and development in the human services.

It was here that I had my first introduction to the joys of hospice service and my love of helping others through the amazing portal called death. I began as a hospice volunteer and received great training from wonderful trainers, and was introduced to clients who were facing death—either their own or a family member's.

I loved being with them and supporting each person in their own unique grieving process. As time went on, and with lots of experience, I developed better sensitivity skills. I wasn't at all daunted or put off by our culture's 'normal' reaction to death—denial. Each individual or family became a wonderful opportunity for me to find new ways to help others deal with the inevitable reality of the end of life, and I in turn learned much from them.

I became the volunteer coordinator of a small hospice society and began training others to work with grieving people. Continuing along my way, I noticed a common thread that ran through almost everyone's death process. Most were grief-ridden and felt like they had not lived the life they had really wanted to. I began to understand the deeper facets of grief.

The grief process continues to fascinate me. What is it all about, really? Why are most North Americans so grief-stricken, and only a rare few not? I began to piece it together with the help of some great teachers, some fantastic books, and a lot of practical experience. Here is a brief recap of some of my discoveries. By the way, grief is a journey, not a cycle. You do not exit the grief journey where you began; you exit a changed and different person.

THE BASIC FACETS OF GRIEF

Though grief is a unique and personal crossing, some aspects of this journey are common. In this section we will review the factors that you will encounter.

THE INITIAL SHOCK

No matter whether the death is expected or not, when your loved one passes on, the reality of the death can be shocking in its finality. It can be especially challenging when the death is unexpected and even more intense in the case of suicide, loss of a child, or murder.

In any case, the shock is real, and along with it comes many physical, emotional, and mental side affects. These reactions are understandable, given it is not only the death of a loved one but the loss of dreams, plans, hopes and a future that 'die' too. All the events we had taken for granted—summer vacations, next Christmas, or the eventual birth of a grandchild are wiped out immediately along with the death of the body.

This initial shock may result in some or all of the following:

- A feeling of low or no energy
- A loss of appetite
- Indulging in distractions like television, smoking, over eating, or drinking
- Loss of sex drive
- A loss of attention to life's details
- No interest in living
- Wandering around in a daze of confusion, not knowing what to do
- Over-thinking the death and how it could have been prevented
- Thinking about suicide

All of these side affects are real and need to be dealt with in a loving and proactive way that supports the individual(s) in embracing, expressing, and completing all their personal reactions to the death. It is important to know that each person's response to death is unique, much like their thumbprint. Everyone will deal with the loss in his or her own way. There is no one formula!

SURVIVOR'S GUILT

In many cases, especially when a parent experiences the death of a child, or in the case of suicide, there can be a reaction referred to as survivor's guilt. When my sister Jody died, I was deeply guilty that I was still alive. I felt that God had made a nasty mistake and had taken the wrong person. I felt that the planet would have been better with Jody here and me dead.

In my experience, this is an aspect I think we often miss, and it is more common than many of us would expect. Guilt is a paralyzing force; it is a self-generated energy that will ultimately block the natural and healthy completion of our grief process. Guilt will hold out love, support, concern and even therapy. It is a force that only the individual can release. Let it go through forgiveness.

If you notice that someone is really stuck in their grief and not making any progress at all, you may want to explore the idea of survivor's guilt with them. It is not supportive, by the way, to use phrases like, "You shouldn't feel so guilty." They *do* feel guilty, and you telling them not to feel that way is counter-productive. We will go into this much more fully in Chapter Six— "Embracing Death – a Survivor's Manual".

For now, know that guilt is real and very much a part of the journey of grief and loss.

EMOTIONAL ROLLER COASTER

If you have ever ridden a roller-coaster, you will appreciate the analogy.

As you are rolling up the first massive hill, there is a feeling of the unexpected; you really don't know what's over the top. When you hit the top of the first huge hill, however, it is an entirely different matter! The shock of the drop is stunning, and then the first sharp corner—holy shit!

The next upward slope brings a short reprieve, and then you go down again—whoosh— another sharp corner, the next gut-wrenching turn, an upside-down twister, cranked around another tight corner, wow the g-force pressure! Up and down, banging all around, faster, sharper, and even more twists and turns, until finally it's over and you find yourself coasting on the flat bottom portion of the ride thinking, "Well, *that* wasn't so bad."

This is how the emotions can go. The shock of the death is stunning—*oh my God!* The first week goes by with a bit of a reprieve before the funeral, then *whoosh!* another full emotion, another reminder of the loss, with all the people mingling together with their own stuff around death, and the twisting and turning of gut-wrenching emotions—the dreams, the unexpected tears, the laughter, the anger, and then the sadness. It doesn't seem to end. *Whoosh!* And then you do it all over again, with more emotional twists and turns.

One emotion that often comes up and deserves individual attention here is anger. Anger is much misunderstood as it is, and at the time of death it becomes even more confusing. Our anger can often be directed at ourselves, or at the one who died, and if not at them, then at others—doctors, nurses, siblings, and sometimes God!

Usually when we feel anger during the grief process we tend to tell ourselves that the feeling is wrong—*You shouldn't be angry with God* and *how could I be angry with my loved one who died?*

I know for a while I was really angry with my sister Jody for dying. It didn't make sense to me and so I tried to stuff it down. How could I be angry with Jody? She was dead, for goodness sake! Yet, there it was—*anger!*

While working with a therapist, I was able to express myself fully and embrace that anger. Once it was expressed and out of the way I could then truly grieve. You see, I was using the anger as a form of denial. It was blocking the deeper feelings of loss and sadness.

Depression is similar. It often stems from the feeling that there is nothing we can do about the death or our feelings of uncontrollable pain.

Many of us, when we are so full of emotions, find ourselves confused and lost, unable to handle the fullness of it all. We can sometime stuff these emotions in an unconscious way to avoid dealing them. Suppression, as is the case with anger, can really abort a healthy grief process. Finding someone we can be expressive with will often open the floodgates of emotions allowing us to move forward.

Over time and with some support, we will all learn how to accept the emotional ups and downs. We will learn that these feelings are natural and healthy to express.

DENIAL DEN

For a while, and for most of us, there is an initial period of denial. You will hear it in the way people speak.

"No, it just can't be so."
"I must be in a nightmare of some kind."
"There must be some mistake."

There are many common forms of denial that we can use. One is outright denial as mentioned above; another is the bargaining phase where we will try our best to make a deal with God to prevent our loved one's death, or even to get them back.

When I had to give the news to my parents about my sister's unexpected death, there was immediate denial from both my Dad and my shocked Mom. Lloyd, my Dad, just could not let the news in. He wasn't prepared for it, nor did he want to accept it. He kept repeating, "It should have been me. It should have been me." My Mom responded with "Are you sure? Isn't there some mistake?"

In both cases, my folks understandably wanted things back to the way they were before I gave them the news. They wanted things back to 'normal'. In my own case, I took the bargaining route, and spent many hours negotiating with God to get my sister back.

I offered all my possessions, my money, my Ping golf clubs, my stock portfolio, and ultimately my own life. This was a strategy, an unconscious one albeit, to turn my life back in time before Jody died. I too wanted things back to 'normal'. I wanted time back so I could say all things I wanted to say to her. I wanted more time to do all the things I wanted to do with her. I wanted more time to tell her how much I loved her.

Ultimately, no matter what strategy we each may choose to deny the death and return things to 'normal', we will not make progress with our own natural grief process until we finally accept the death as reality.

I remember the day I finally 'got' that Jody was dead and that, no matter what I did, she was not coming back to life. The absolute reality of it was crushing. I would never be able to hug her again. She was *dead*. And yet in the midst of the pain of the real loss, I became free and able to move forward without her with me. I was able to hold her in my memory bank—not in my denial den!

FACING YOUR OWN MORTALITY

One of the issues that pops up almost immediately when given the news of a loved one's impending death or their actual death is the certainty of our own. We may be conscious of its inevitability, but on many levels we are blind to it. It lurks in the background of our mind and body, often acting out in a subconscious fashion.

If you leaf back a few pages and review the fear of death section you will understand why facing your own death is so important. Here is the thing: if you haven't confronted your own death, how on earth can you help a friend or family member face theirs?

You can't!

Each time you walk into the room where someone is terminally ill, your own death will silently rear its head. Not having faced your own passing, you will unconsciously steer towards denial, hope, or some other avoidance. You likely won't say or do things that are based on the reality of the situation. You will say things like:

"I'm sure they are close to a cure for cancer!"

"Its not your time to go."

"I know you will be one of the 13 percent that make it through."

What I want you to understand here is that I am not talking about giving in or being gloomy. I am also clear that the overly-optimistic approach isn't sensible. In a way, it's like playing poker. The cards are what they are, and three of a kind beats a pair no matter how you try to look at it.

The same holds true in life and death. The cards are what they are, so let's put them all on the table face up and deal with what is in front of us. Face the facts—you are going to die too one day! No one has ever gotten off this planet alive! The more real you can be with your own death, the more of a genuine help you can be for a friend or family member that is dying.

Here is a gem for you:

The degree to which you can accept your own death
is the same degree you will embrace and live your own life!

In our world of opposites we need to embrace *both* sides of the coin. If you cannot embrace your death, you simply won't fully embrace your life. You will hold back a touch, just in case. You will not risk as fully as you could, and you will play it safe. Have a look at "Other types of deaths" below and you will see what I mean.

Remember a time when you knew you should quit your job? You knew internally that you were done with it, and yet you held on, denied your need to move on, and failed to acknowledge your job was dead. How about the death of a relationship? Do you notice a similar denial pattern? Yet you didn't want to suffer the reality that the relationship was really over.

OTHER TYPES OF DEATHS

- Loss of a job
- End of a relationship
- A miscarriage or abortion
- Close of a day
- Death of your bank account
- Loss of family pet
- Giving up of a dream
- End of an age or era
- Loss of mobility or a faculty (sight, hearing, etc.)

Death tends to get focused on a physical death or loss of the body. Yes, this is perceived as the big one, and yet we can prepare for our body's death by understanding that these 'other' deaths are a similar experience. Something *was,* and *now it is no longer,* a loss occurred. In Chapter Six, "Embracing Death—A Survivor's Manual", I will share some great daily, weekly, and yearly practices you can do easily and joyfully— practices that will help you embrace your very own bodily death.

NOTABLE DATES

You will discover as you move along your own unique path of grief and bereavement that, from time to time, you will be reminded of the loved one who died. Sometimes these feelings of sadness or melancholy will sneak up on you with what seems like no notice. However, if you look closely, you may realize that an important date connected to your loved one is just around the corner. Typically these occasions are:

- A birthday
- An anniversary
- A regular vacation time
- A special day of the week, month or year
- Holiday times like Thanksgiving, Christmas, the New Year, and Easter
- Spring break
- Major sporting events like the Stanley Cup or Super Bowl

There can be many more occasions depending on your cultural and religious background, and these regularly-occurring dates are often grief triggers. These are times you used to share with your loved one—common times when celebrations or family gatherings took place. These are special occasions you associate with being together with the friend or family member who died.

You will notice them much more profoundly for the first year or two. Over time, the intensity will subside, and yet you still may miss the friend or family member. I remember the first two or three years after my sister Jody died, especially at Christmas, as her birthday was December 23rd, which gave us *two* reminders that she was no longer with us! I shed lots of tears that first year, and the second year, too, for that matter. Now at Christmas, when I am filling out a card for the local hospice society's Christmas Tree of Life, I remember her fully—sometimes with a tear of joy, and other times not; either way, I still have deep and fond memories of Jody.

You know your own notable dates, and can do some advanced preparation in order to be ready for the emotional response that may occur at these times.

© 2007 barbara cameron pix

YOU ARE ON THE RIGHT PATH

ACCEPTANCE

Though it may seem a long way down the road, acceptance of the death of your loved one finally does arrive. This can be a time of some confusion and a bit of guilt as you start to feel alive again. Fun, joy, pleasure, and maybe even romance start to become more of a possibility as the primary reactions to death have been fully expressed and released.

In most cases it is not like a declaration, such as "Today I have accepted my husband's death." It is more like a gradual noticing. It may seem that all of a sudden the emotional roller-coaster has settled. A clue may be, for example, that you have gone out with friends and had a good time without a thought of your loved one's death.

You may even find one day that your memories are sweet and do not bring up such big emotions; you can be at familiar places without looking over your shoulder to see if your loved one is there.

This is a matter of the heart, a matter of time, and a matter of a real good-bye.

ANOTHER ASPECT OF DEATH: PRE-DEATH REGRETS

I spent years as a hospice volunteer and worked closely with people dying. I heard many regrets over the years from people closing in on their death—some unusual ones for sure. Here are a few that people shared with me over the years:

I wish I'd had the courage to live my life, and not live the life others expected of me. Many folks spend a lifetime doing their best to make people around them happy. Many of us put those things we really want to do on the back burner. We forfeit the life we really want to live in order to live a life we think will gain us the approval of those important people around us—approval from Mom, Dad, or our spouse, or perhaps kids, peers and society.

It is a common disappointment to get to the end of life only to discover we have run out of time, leaving unfulfilled dreams behind.

I wish I hadn't worked so hard. If I had a penny for each time I heard this one I would most certainly be a millionaire by now! All that time people spend working hard so that, upon retiring, they will finally be free and able to do those things which bring them happiness. They think, *One more year, a few more dollars in the retirement fund, then I can relax and enjoy my life.* Often that extra year doesn't arrive, and the next few dollars no longer matter; our health is so poor that we can no longer enjoy the dream. Delayed gratification is not worth the cost.

I wish I'd had the courage to express myself more fully. This speaks to how we hold ourselves back from really expressing ourselves in order to be part of a family, community, group, or team. It is a painful recognition when we realize we didn't give our fullest to our own life. We held our truest expression back because we were afraid to be left alone, put down, or ridiculed.

I wish I had stayed in touch with my friends and family. Many of us get so busy in life that we tend to focus on what is right in front of us, oftentimes excluding friends and family. It is most often recognized that, at the end of life, relationships are all that really mattered, and we regret all the time we spent doing other things. Many of us realize at the end of life that it is only these relationships that we take with us when we die. All else we leave behind. Oftentimes at the end of life we haven't the time or capacity to get in touch with all those folks that are important to us.

I wish that I had expressed the happiness I felt. This is a sneaky one and yet very common. It links to the regret many of us have that we didn't express ourselves fully. Most of us carry around the belief that we don't deserve to be happy, even though we feel it. Most of us hold it back, especially when other around us aren't so happy. At the end of life we begin to understand that we were happy all along, and we regret deeply that we didn't share that joy with those close to us.

These regrets are real for the grieving person. It is good to simply receive them and validate their feelings. You will find more hints on how to deal with regrets a little later in the book.

THE OTHER SIDE OF THE DEATH COIN

Now, for a real twist, lets take a look at the upside of death; there are actually some benefits and good points. This may seem odd, and yet if embraced for its benefits as well as its losses, we can have a much more full and balanced approach to life and death.

Death can really help us examine our daily existence and causes us to evaluate how fully and deeply we really are living. Having death sitting on your shoulder as a gentle and consistent reminder of the lack of permanence of life can support each one of us to live with more passion and inspiration. Viewed as a friend, death can remind us not to put off until tomorrow the love we can share today, the dreams we can live today, and the differences we can make today.

Death is the big equalizer! I have seen many, and it didn't matter how much money the person had, what their social status was, or what they did for a living. It didn't matter what color, race, gender, age, or culture. We come in the same way: birth. We all go out the same way: death.

Death pushes itself into life, and if you allow it to, it gives it meaning. Many of us take life for granted until it is too late. Embracing death can enhance the value of life and help us all appreciate life moment to moment with even more gratitude.

Death teaches us to live with the unknown. In this age of technology and information we tend to think we need to know everything, to be able to control our lives and keep ourselves and our family and friends safe. Imagine knowing before your life began how it would go; wouldn't that take the fun, excitement, and magic out of it? Learning to deal with the unknown and letting go of the uncontrollable will inject new joy, passion, and mystery into your life.

As it is often said when one door closes another one always opens. Focusing on the closing door means that we tend not to see the one that is opening. When death arrives, remember to stay present to both sides of the door as best you can.

Nothing ever ceases to exist. Death is incubation in the field of potentiality till the next leap of creativity.—Deepak Chopra

CHAPTER THREE

Other Cultures Do It Differently

The Rituals of Death in the World Around Us

It's only when we truly know and understand that we have a limited time on earth—and that we have no way of knowing when our time is up—that we will begin to live each day to the fullest, as if it was the only one we had.—Elisabeth Kubler-Ross

© 2009 barbara cameron pix

YOU CAN PAINT A NEW PICTURE OF DEATH

I took a trip to Bali in the fall of 2010 ,and amongst other things, was struck by the way death was embraced in their culture. We were touring different sacred sites, geographic areas, and generally exploring life in that exquisite place. From the rice fields in the countryside to shopping stalls in Ubud, as well as a shaman's home in Mas and cafés in Denpasar, we saw lots of wonderful people and places. The most profound event, though, was the cremation ceremony of one of the Royal Family members.

We were invited by the guide who was supporting our tour to come and 'enjoy' the ceremony and all the activities that were common in a cremation. So we did. When we arrived at the site I was astounded at what I saw: happy people were everywhere, dancing, praying, eating, and celebrating. It was so not what I expected. There were holy people there leading prayers and meditation, business men, students, children, elders, couples, singles, and tourists by the hundreds. It seemed like everyone was welcome to join the celebration, and celebrate they did!

There was a parade with bands, dancers, floats and clowns, tons of music, confetti, and balloons. It was so joyous and colorful that I was certain it was a statutory holiday. Being somewhat confused by it all, I asked a local merchant what the heck was going on.

He told me it was all created to give the one who has died a great send-off. The noise, color, and music were all designed to disorient the spirit of the dead person in order that they 'get lost' from their family and friends and can more easily let go of the life they just completed. Sometimes grief and mourning would keep the spirit 'connected' to their loved ones and slow their journey to the other side, so the constant dancing and celebrating were created intentionally to support the transition from life to death. What a different and fascinating way to say good-bye!

Our trip to Bali and this celebration of a life well-lived inspired me to write *When Death Speaks.* Another example of the dual-sided coin of death and birth: a woman died in Bali, and the seed for my book was born in Canada.

I was reminded of the many adventures I have had traveling around the world. I recalled trips to Peru, India, Egypt, Kenya, Mexico and Costa Rica, and remembered many instances where death was being 'lived' differently than in North America.

There are some unique ways in which cultures around the world think, feel, and deal with death. This is not a formal report on death beliefs and practices around the world; it is designed to open your minds and hearts to different perspectives other cultures hold dear.

It is not about finding the 'right' way, for I believe each of us has *our own right way.* I intend to paint a tapestry of death celebrations so each of us can find our own way with a slightly broader and more informed perspective. I invite you to enjoy these stories.

I developed many lasting friendships on my travels and have asked some of my them to write about the different cultural approaches to death with which they are familiar. I am happy they sent me some wonderful additions to this chapter.

A dear friend, adventurer, and author Stephen Mehler travelled with me in Egypt several years ago. I was taken by his enthusiasm for Egypt and its history. I was fascinated by his love and curiosity of all things Egyptian and his grasp of the historic details. He also had a passion for the spiritual aspects of that great land. He agreed to write a short piece on death from his experience and understanding of the spiritual culture of Egypt. Here is his contribution:

DEATH IN ANCIENT EGYPT

Stephen S. Mehler, MA

Dozens of books are published every year, in many languages, on some aspect of the culture of ancient Egypt. The specific topic of death in ancient Egypt, from the philosophy of, to practices, rituals, and attitudes towards, are usually found in every one of these books. But, as one who has studied the civilization(s) found under the general rubric "ancient Egypt" for over forty-three years, I have noted that the majority of what has been written about death and all its ramifications in that ancient culture to be superficial and not adequately researched or understood.

I was fortunate to have been a student, disciple, and friend to a master of the wisdom traditions of ancient Egypt. Abd'El Hakim Awyan (1926-2008) was an archaeologist, Egyptologist and senior tour guide in Egypt for over fifty-six years. He was also an indigenous wisdom-keeper and a master of the oral traditions of his native country. Together, he and I created the discipline of Khemitology, to differ from the academic field of Egyptology—*Khemit* being the ancient term for the civilization.

My two books, *The Land of Osiris*, and *From Light into Darkness*, document this information. Hakim presented the thesis that a previous, highly-advanced indigenous civilization called KMT (Khemit) existed thousands of years before recognized academic dates for the term "ancient Egypt", over 10,000 years ago, and they were the peoples who built the pyramids and carved the Sphinx.

Among the many profound things that Hakim taught was that there was a far different concept of death that was held by the ancients than has ever been brought forward. Very early in my tutelage with Hakim, he presented the teaching that the very ancient Khemitians (Egyptians), over 10,000 years ago, did *not* have a word in their language for death. They used the phrases "Westing," or "going to the West," for the release of the physical form, but did not see the body as the total existence. The end of the physical envelope was not the cessation of consciousness.

Hakim further taught that all moves in cycles—in some parts of the whole cycle we are in higher states of consciousness than in others. It was the fall from full and total consciousness that caused people to question what happens after the end of the physical form—no longer in full consciousness, people lost the connection from the physical to the non-physical; this led to the rise of priesthoods who promoted the idea of the fear of physical death, and "religion" was born. This new system introduced the concepts of "soul," "afterlife," and God as Creator. Hakim profoundly taught that these concepts did not exist to the ancients.

Religion started in ancient Egypt ca. 4000 to 2000 BCE, and has formed the template for all modern religions, from Judaism to Christianity and Islam. All practices, rituals, and concepts around death in those religions began in so-called "Dynastic" Egypt. A key understanding that Hakim left us has come down in modern religious practices. In the last eight thousand years, the climate in Northern Africa has been hot and dry—desert conditions. Preservation of the body became a central idea in this new religion, and was made possible by the climatic desert conditions, thus the major concept of Resurrection was instituted—that there was an immortal soul that could return to a preserved body, and the practice of mummification was born.

In ancient Asia, Hakim taught, the climate stayed hot and moist, which was not ideal for preserving bodies. The ancient Asians conceived of the concept of Reincarnation—destroying the body through cremation, but with the guarantee of the soul returning to a new body!

Both concepts became the basis of the afterlife in all modern religions. But the key understanding of the very ancient Africans we call Khemitians was that *there is no death;* this is not understood by the majority of people today. But it is what the ancients realized: being in full consciousness, that Death is an illusion, as are God and soul. The physical form was just a vehicle for temporary residence of spirit, upon "Westing" consciousness returned to source—always existing, with no beginning, and no end.

Stephen, thank you for your contribution!

MOTHER INDIA AND HER WAYS

I have travelled to India three times since 2004 and each time I have been struck by how openly Hindu families handle death. I was shocked by how public their ceremonies were. Families carried the body of a loved one to a funeral fire on the side of the Ganges River; dead bodies of the poor lay on the sidewalks near the ghats waiting for donations so they too could be cremated; families scooped up the ashes, spreading them on the river. It all seemed so unrestricted and raw.

In my ongoing travels to India, especially Varanasi, I noticed that death was a fundamental part of Indian life. It was everywhere and not at all hidden or shied away from. It was celebrated as an opening to another life or realm. Dead bodies were part of the landscape of Varanasi, with families washing the body and preparing it for cremation, carrying the body to the funeral pyre, and placing the ashes in the river Ganges. Family members, young and old, were all involved in the celebration of a life lived. I became curious about why there was such a difference in how death was treated in India and how we 'managed' it here in Canada.

On my third trip to this great continent I was traveling with a group of about thirty people. We were again in Varanasi. The evening before we had watched the Arti, the daily ritual, the celebration of life and light. Early the next morning, some of us were wandering in the back streets and alleys close to the funeral pyres. We wound our way through the ever-narrowing roadways and back alleys towards the river. Sunsets were always spectacular and we were also excited to watch the sunrise over the River Ganges. We turned a corner, and then out of nowhere, we stumbled right into the centre of all cremations!

It was a small nook tucked under an overhang surrounded by firewood. There was a fire pit in the centre with a small fire burning. Smoke drifted past us and through the alleys and walkways. A stoic gentleman tended the fire. It was a most sacred place. We had found the spot that was home to the fire from which all funeral pyres were lit. Legend has it that this fire had been burning for 5,000 years! It was absolutely breathtaking. Those I wandered with that morning slowly went their own ways. I stayed behind, though, and spent the better part of the day there. I witnessed several ceremonies and was staggered by the open and natural way death was attended to. In Varanasi, death is holy and auspicious, and it is seen as natural, unavoidable, and certain. It is welcomed as a long-awaited guest.

As I explored the Hindu approach to death, I noticed that the entire family was actively involved in most of the ceremonies, including the children! You see, in India, they believe that their children do not need to be sheltered from death. Even to this day, Indian families do their best to bring the loved one home to die where the entire family takes turns sitting the vigil so that the one who is passing is never alone.

There are many pieces to the rituals that families go through before and after a loved one dies. Here are some I found most interesting:

Most often the body is returned home from the hospital if the death happened there; it is not embalmed and nothing is removed from the body. Family members and relatives are all invited to bid farewell by singing and chanting.

The family takes full care of the body, washing, dressing, and preparing for the funeral fire. The body is laid on the pyre ,and generally the eldest son starts the fire. Once lit, the family leaves and returns home. All share in the cleaning of the home. Within twelve hours, family members return to the fire and collect the ashes that are then spread on the Ganges or another spiritually important river.

There can be very complex rituals associated with death that sometimes last for a year, marking particularly important dates and events. It can be a lengthy process.

So there you have it: in a very general way, that is how open and public death is in India. What a difference to our way here in North America.

Being a fortunate fellow, I have also had the pleasure of also traveling in South America. I learned much from my experiences there. I have twice travelled through Peru and adventured through the sacred valley that contained such sites as Machu Pichu. Diego and Don Jorge, two of the great shaman and teachers of the area, spent a great deal of time with all of us on these spiritual adventure tours. They taught us much about the Peruvian culture and its sacred traditions and ceremonies. I was moved by the simplicity and earthiness of lifestyle in the sacred valleys of Peru, as well as the peoples' connection with all things spiritual.

We didn't spend any time talking about death while in Peru, so I thought I would do some research. It was intriguing to see the unique ways in which Peruvians dealt with death. How was their culture different from that of India and North America?

Kenneth Kensinger wrote a book entitled *How Real People Ought to Live: The Cashinahua of Eastern Peru*. This book describes in great detail the lives of those who are considered the people of the Amazon.

The Cashinahua believe that our human body is maintained by key spirits: the three primary ones being spirits of the body, the dreams, and the eye, the primary spirit being the eye spirit. In North America, you may hear this 'spirit' referred to as the glimmer in someone's eye!

Their belief is that when the eye spirit leaves for good, so does the soul. When the light is dimming in the eyes of the one passing on, a period of mourning begins. When the person is fading, the family, neighbors, and sometimes the entire village begin singing and chanting to help ease the soul out of the body and send it on its way.

Once the person is dead, the body is wrapped in cloth and buried with their personal possessions and sacred objects as close to the village as possible. Once buried, the mourning simply stops; family and village life carries on as normal.

Short and sweet.

So that is Peru. Let's move on to one of my other experiences:

MEXICO AND THE MAYA

Back in the fall of 2009, I spent two weeks traveling through the sacred sites of the Maya, exploring ancient pyramids, jungles, waterfalls, and hidden caves. It was a spectacular time rich in experiences and teachings of the Mayan culture.

Don Miguel, our guide, took me under his wing and taught me much about the shamanic realms so common to the Maya. He taught me about shape-shifting, receiving information from the Great Mystery, and how to take everything in life as a teaching. I was fascinated by the Mayan approach to life, the beauty of their art, the simplicity of their view of life, and the brilliance of their engineering.

Don Miguel and I didn't take the time to speak about the Mayan approach to death as we were way too busy exploring how they lived life. So I checked in with my Mexican friend and colleague Alexandra who suggested I read Charles Gallenkamp's wonderful book entitled *Maya: The Riddle and Rediscovery of a Lost Civilization.*

In this book, Gallenkamp spent some time discussing the way the Maya approached death. Some of their practices are very interesting, and I wanted to share them with you. You will notice yet another unique approach to such a common occurrence—death.

The Maya are thought of as a religious people, and death rituals became an important part of their life. They developed many traditions to commemorate the recently deceased and worship long-departed ancestors. Interestingly, the Maya greatly respected death, yet they were taught to fear it, and grieved deeply for the dead. They also believed that certain deaths were more important than others. People who died by suicide, sacrifice, and in battle were sent directly to heaven. The guilty and evil suffered eternally in Xilbalba, the Mayan version of hell.

There was also a belief that death was a journey, with the chance of rebirth. It was believed that certain people, important to their lineage, became deities that acted as guides for the surviving members of their current family and many future generations.

Traditionally the Mayan dead were laid to rest with corn placed in their mouth. Maize (corn) was important in this culture, and is a symbol of rebirth. It was also food for the dead for the trip to the otherworld. A jade or stone bead was placed in the mouth and served as currency for the journey.

These people associated the color red with death and rebirth, and often covered graves and skeletal remains with cinnabar. The bodies were wrapped in cotton mantles before being buried. Graves faced north or west, in the directions of the Maya heavens, and others were located in caves, believed to be entrances to the underworld.

There have been many archaeological discoveries of amazing tombs where a city's most important ruler was buried. These aristocrats were placed in mausoleums at the bottom of a funerary pyramid that consisted of nine stair-like platforms. These stepped landings symbolized the nine layers of the underworld. Other temples were constructed with thirteen vaults symbolizing the layers of the heavens in Maya cosmology.

The tombs were filled with precious goods, including fine polychrome pottery, effigy figurines, jade and marble pieces, masks, mushroom figures, obsidian, exotic shells and valuable stones.

Commoners, however, were buried near or under their houses. These graves did not have extensive burial offerings, but often contained objects that identified the loved one. Burial practices of the Maya changed over the course of time, and eventually cremation became more common than elaborate burial sites.

It is very interesting to note that death practices alter over time. Though the principles are constant, the how-to or the rituals change and evolve. We here in North America are in the process of changing how we approach the rituals of death, just as all other more ancient cultures have done.

These are several looks at different cultures and their approach to death. I encourage you to read a few more accounts of death ceremonies to broaden your knowledge of how varied they can be, as it will help you to create your own personal ceremonies for you and your loved ones.

A man's dying is more the survivors' affair than his own.—Thomas Mann

© 2012 barbara cameron pix

YOU DON'T HAVE TO DO THIS ALONE

CHAPTER FOUR

Beginning the New Conversation
Real Life Stories of Death

Death is a very real experience. Usually, we do not connect with a sense of reality. If we have an accident—or whatever happens in our lives—we do not regard it as a real experience, even though it may hurt us. It is real to us as far as pain and physical damages are concerned, but still it's not real for us because we immediately look at it in terms of how it could be otherwise. There's always the idea of first aid or some other redeeming aspect of the situation. If you're talking to a dying friend or relative, you should transmit the idea that death is a real experience, rather than that it's just a joke and that the person could get better. We should help the dying person to understand that death is real. "Death and the Sense of Experience" in Crazy Wisdom —Chogyam Trungpa Rinopche

Chogyam Trungpa Rinopche is a world known spiritual master who has written many books over the years. A friend of mine sent the above quote along for me to have a look at and, it fits really well in this chapter as an introduction into the reality of death and near-death experiences of friends of mine. These real-life stories may help you begin to see how all of us at one time or another will face death head on, each in our own unique way.

These amazing people want to share their experiences so we can all learn more about the mystery of death and near-death. They all made a contribution to this book so others might have a broader understanding and a more graceful and open approach to death that we will all face one way or another. I am deeply grateful to each one of these remarkable individuals.

RUSSELL SCOTT

A dear and long-lost friend of mine, Russell Scott, showed up in my life recently with a brilliant story about how a near-death experience has fundamentally changed his life. He had written a couple of blogs on his web site *www.truesourceseminars.com* and they struck me as potentially wonderful additions to my book. Russell had suffered a burst blood vessel in his head and was facing his death in a very physical and dramatic way. Thankfully he has survived and is able to share his journey with us.

I contacted Russell immediately and asked if he would be up for having his story in this book. He said, "Yes, of course." So here is the result of our conversations and emails.

"So what happened Russell?" I asked.

"Well, it is a bit of a story ,Stephen. On the evening of November 7th, I went to emergency at Guelph General Hospital with the worst migraine imaginable. On a scale of 1-10 it was about 100. I felt as if my head was going to explode. It felt like it was like a huge gaseous pumpkin on fire yet the rest of my body was cold. It was the weirdest sensation. Everything below my neck was shivering and above I was sweating."

Russell continued: "After the admitting nurse examined me, I spent four and a half hours in agony without a nurse or a doctor checking in on me. Thank God for my partner Heather who asked for a towel and gave me cold compresses and her love for the whole time. I could have had a stroke, unattended, and died."

"So it was darn serious," I chipped in. 'What happened next?"

"Well, oddly enough, somewhere in the midst of this trauma, while lying on a hospital gurney in the hallway, I noticed my mind," he said, still somewhat surprised by his realization.

He continued: "I observed my mind doing it's "futurizing" thing: looking into the past for disastrous similar events and projecting them into the future. It sounded something like this:"

'Remember the time you were in the hospital, when you were two years old, remember the concussion you had playing football, remember your friend who died when he got hit by a baseball bat. Russell, you are going to die; you'll be disabled for the rest of your life; you'll be stuck in the hospital for six weeks and nobody will visit; you'll be abandoned; nobody will ever love you again'...It just went on and on and on, making up all kinds of things," he said, somewhat embarrassed.

"Tell me some more, will you?" I encouraged.

Not needing much encouragement, Russell continued on. "I saw my mind for the nervous fool it actually was, making up everything under the sun it could possibly disastrously imagine; it was full of negative beliefs, erroneous points of view, unproven conclusions with false evidence, randomly ascribing meaning to the current situation. Exhausted, I finally asked my mind:

'Hey, mind of this Russell dude, how do I know that anything you are predicting is true or will come to pass? The day isn't over yet.'

Oddly enough, my mind responded like a nervous witness with a false story being interrogated in court:

'Well sir, you see, well I, what I really mean is, golly gee, I know it could maybe be true, what I am thinking could happen is...ah, hum...well the truth be told, I'm making it all up.'

And *poof!* Like a stupid genie, my mind vanished, and all that was left was me and the pain," he asserted.

"Russell, what did you learn from all of this?" I asked.

"I realized in that moment," he said, "that I could make up anything I wanted about the pain because the future really was not set. I had no idea what would happen in the future because it is not dependent on the past."

"I remember thinking to myself that maybe there is wisdom inherent in just being with the pain as it is, without any imposition of positive or negative meaning. So I chose to just be me, with the pain…just be me with the bare excruciating experience of pain…with nothing in between."

Russell was inspired to get the full idea across to me so he continued on.

"I saw I am separate from the pain. I felt the pain, but just because I felt it, it did not mean I was it. I was not identified with it. Pain did not define me. My body did not define me. The lack of attention by the nurses did not define me, nor did whatever my mind made up. In fact, nothing defined me. Death or life did not define me. I may die but I would still exist…just me without a body.

And in all of this I had a choice independent of my mind. In this situation of possibly dying I could choose anything I wanted. Being at choice is fundamental to my true nature and I am free. I could choose to throw up, trash the nurses' station, fart just for fun, leave or die… whatever.

So I chose to live…to love my partner who loves me dearly and to base my new life from living and loving more in my heart than in my mind," he concluded.

"Wow, you got all that from a burst blood vessel," I commented

"Yes, and what is more exciting is what I learned from the other patients in the hospital room with me," he said, tempting me to ask the next obvious question.

No surprise—I took the bait and said, "Well, do tell!"

Being a great storyteller, Russell leapt at the opportunity to share even more about what else he had learned while facing his own death in the presence of others who were doing just the same.

"There was this gasping man across from me. He was in a semi-coma on intravenous feeding and a respirator. About every sixth inhalation he'd gasp desperately for air as if it were his last breath. I remember counting. It was regular. He looked to be about eighty years old.

He was a puzzle to me.

I couldn't understand why a man near the end of his life—who was in so much distress— would want to live. Why didn't he just give up and die? It seemed like maybe he was just afraid to die, but when I put my attention on his gasping I detected no fear in his paroxysms. There was more yearning than fear. Though I was in a hell of a lot better shape than this man, I felt some affinity with him.

It wasn't that he was afraid to die. He was afraid not to live. His gasping was a grasping for life. He hadn't finished his living. He hadn't fully experienced what it was like to almost die and come back to life and feel the simple gratitude of just being in a body and being able to:

> Gaze through human eyes out the window, watching the wind blowing the leaves across the parking lot…

> Enjoy the everyday pleasure of looking into his children's and partner's eyes, seeing the unspoken love behind all the speaking…

> Appreciate the blessing of having a calling and a purpose in life and struggling to fulfill it…

Like him, I was afraid that I would die without fully engaging in why I was here. And it became clear to me that the tragedy of life is not that we die—it's that we do not fully live.

It made me sad to contemplate how many people die before their time in life, not due to some illness or accident, but because they bring on these calamities because it is too painful to live their lives with no meaning.

They miss that the simple purpose of life is just living it fully."

Russell and I sat quietly for a moment, just allowing this beautiful realization to be. I thanked Russell for his time and his heartfelt stories, as well as his willingness to be a part of my book. I am glad I know him and that our friendship transcends time.

PETER GARRETT

My brother has faced cancer twice in the past couple of years and it was a challenging adventure for him. The beauty of it all, though, has been the growing relationship between the two of us; we are much closer now that we ever have been. What a gift!

When I began writing this book, I thought of Peter's journey with cancer, and imagined it would be a helpful and inspiring story for you. I called Peter and asked him if he would consider writing a piece for my new book. He thought it over, taking his time to make sure is was the right thing for him and the right thing for the book. He said 'Yes,' so here is his contribution with only a few edits—after all, an older brother has some unearned rights!

"When my brother asked me to write a chapter for his new book, I asked him 'why?' and he said that he thought my 'near-death' experience (as he called it) might help others. When I asked him how long, he said between 2,000 to 3,000 words. Seriously? First of all, I'm Irish. Secondly, I used to be a lawyer (but it's okay—I saw the light and got out early) and he wants me to use only 3,000 words? I suppose in some alternate universe that could happen.

However, the sesquipedalian gene runs strong in my family. So, with absolutely no apologies to Stephen, here goes...

I was born in 1954, the fourth of five children, in Montreal just before the start of the Canadiens string of five consecutive Stanley Cups (still a record more than fifty years later). Sports was a strong theme growing up in our household. My brother and I were always involved in sports, hockey being the main one. Montreal brought that out in people back then.

I am a father of three boys, an ex-husband, and a current husband. I work for the Canadian Government, and have been a laborer and lawyer amongst other things. I never smoked; I drank sparingly, have eaten well and led as good a life as I knew how. I won't bore you with all the other mundane historical pieces of my life as they all somehow become much less important given the story I am about to share with you. With this unsatisfyingly short synopsis of my life, let's begin the part Stephen wants me to get to.

It was October 2008 – my annual physical. Towards the end, I pointed out a lump in my right groin and asked my family physician to check it out, explaining that I had had a similar one on my left groin about fifteen years earlier and it had turned out to be a benign fat deposit. I wasn't at all concerned this time as I assumed it would be the same kind of thing. However, the doctor was concerned and suggested that it was likely cancerous, and that I should consult the surgeon at the hospital. I was skeptical. The two lumps, to my mind (me being such a great medical specialist and all), looked the same. The previous one had been excised and sent for testing and came back as benign. Accordingly, I remained unconcerned.

Fast-forwarding to February 2009 and my meeting with the surgeon at Whitehorse General Hospital. He told me that he was 99 percent certain that I had cancer. Okay—that got my attention. The staff at the hospital told me there was an opening the next day for a biopsy as a patient had just cancelled an appointment—otherwise there would be a four to six-month wait. I told them that didn't work for me I had to do a presentation the following day so they put me on a wait list.

However, on the way back to the office something unexpected happened. Halfway up the Two Mile Hill I started crying and said out loud, 'I don't want to die'. I have never been overly comfortable with emotions so this was a bit disconcerting and it was also good to realize that at the deepest level of my being, I was choosing life. I called the hospital as soon as I got back to the office and booked the available appointment for the biopsy.

It took an extremely long month to get the results back.

The day finally arrived, the call was holding for me. Unfortunately the doctor had a thick accent and I was unable to understand what he was saying. I called the medical office and asked them to have someone I could understand call me—after all, this was somewhat important to me and I wanted a degree of certainty about the results. Five minutes later, I received another call, and to my surprise it was the same doctor. After several minutes of not understanding anything he was saying, I finally said: 'Doctor, I am sorry but I cannot understand what you are saying. It may be the phone connection, it may be me but I need to be clear about the results. So, I am going to ask you a question and I want you to respond with a single word only. Do I have cancer?' The answer was crystal clear… YES!

That set into motion a series of tests to determine the extent and location of the cancer, culminating with a very strong 'suggestion' from my oncologist that I immediately undergo radiation therapy. He explained the cancer was neither widespread nor very aggressive. He also said that I was young and healthy (which immediately catapulted him to the top of my Christmas card list), and that this was the ideal time to 'stop this thing'— this thing being Non-Hodgkin's Lymphoma.

At the time, I was 'tele-working' from my home in the Kootenays. The closest cancer clinic in British Columbia was in Kelowna, a half day's drive from my place. The arrangements were made. I was to begin radiation treatments in four months—July 2009. I felt optimistic and got on with my life while awaiting the treatments.

I arrived the Sunday before the treatments were to start and checked into the cancer care lodge immediately adjacent to the cancer clinic. The lodge was a godsend as hotels in the Okanagan in the middle of summer can be pricey. The lodge was not only affordably-priced—it also included all meals and had a nurse on staff. In addition, there was an incredible group of volunteers without whom the lodge could not function.

I checked in and got unpacked in my half of the room (turns out I was to have a roommate) and then went down to the cafeteria for dinner. I grabbed a tray and headed towards the line-up and stopped halfway there, frozen in place.

It finally hit me that my cancer was real.

I was going to get my first radiation treatment the next morning. All this time, I thought that I had been handling things well—more likely I had been at least somewhat in denial. I could not move. I felt overwhelmed, terrified, and alone.

A hand gently touched my shoulder. I heard a voice asking me if I was okay. It was one of the other residents of the lodge. Slowly I turned to her and said, 'It just hit me that this is all real.' I didn't elaborate, nor did I have to. The compassionate look on her face told me she understood exactly what I was saying. She asked me if I would like to join her and her friends at their table. I gratefully accepted. She stayed with me while I went through the line-up for dinner and then walked me back to the table.

Though seemingly a little thing, it meant so much to me (and still does) that she recognized what I was going through and chose to help me.

The group was entirely composed of women. We did the round of introductions and they quickly returned to their conversation. They discussed a variety of things, including their upcoming treatments, but the tone was sur-prisingly upbeat and positive. I heard nothing along the lines of 'poor me' or 'why is this happening to me?' It turns out that this was common for almost all of the residents of the lodge.

It was not that they didn't realize the seriousness of the situation: it was more as though they chose not to give away their power to it. They all chose to make the best of it. During the entire length of my stay, I met only two people who focused on the negative. I was inspired by those who chose the positive route so much so that I chose the positive road too! Now, this is not to say that they didn't have bad days; we all did. It was just that, overall, we chose life and to focus on the positive aspects of being alive. I remained part of the group for my entire stay at the clinic.

One night in the dessert line-up, I noticed one of the women filling her plate with pie, ice cream and other sweet things. I didn't say anything, but must have raised my eyebrows in surprise. She turned to me and said, 'Peter, I have cancer. No one is going to tell me what I can or can't eat!' I laughed, somewhat embarrassed, and asked if I could borrow that line from time to time. When she left on her 'Emancipation Day' a couple of weeks later, I gave her a gift from the local Winners store: an ice cream serving set.

I started my treatments on a Monday morning, and they were to be done daily, Monday to Friday. Thankfully I got weekends off. The first day, they made three small tattoos on my body so that they could triangulate the machine in order to radiate exactly the same area each time. Trying more to quell my nervousness than to make them laugh, I asked whether I could choose my tattoo pattern to which they said, 'No. It is really only three small dots.' I asked if I could choose a color only to be rebuffed again.

After they tattooed me, I had my first treatment. The machine was enor-mous and looked like something straight out of a Star Wars movie. Most of the session was spent lining up the machine with the tattoos. The actual radia-tion portion seemed rather brief. I actually felt nothing during the treatments themselves. I discovered that the side effects would kick in later. This became the central part of each day in relation to which all other things were second-ary. There were set meal times and, except for really bad days, I rarely missed a meal, and almost always sat with the group I had met on the first night.

The radiation technicians were excellent, and were both professional and friendly. They were also a great source of help in me understanding what my body was going through. They would recommend things for the simpler side effects, and referred me to my oncologist for the more complex affects.

On weekends, I would drive the five-and-a-half hours home to Wynell to reconnect with my wife April. Fortunately, one of the other residents, Bev, had given me a gel seat to make the drive more endurable (at least as far as one of the side effects was concerned). The two days always passed far too quickly, and by Sunday night I was back at the lodge in Kelowna.

During my time at the clinic I began to consider the possibility that this cancer might have happened for a reason, so I began to explore what that might be. The cancer clinic had arranged weekly meditation sessions, and one of the women at my table, Darla, had asked me whether I would like to attend. I readily agreed and quite enjoyed them.

After doing a lot of reading and meditation, I came to the conclusion that I had spent far too much of my life being a Type A personality, a perfectionist, and a bit of a workaholic. I was reminded about a cliché: *nobody on their deathbed ever says: 'I wish I had spent more time in the office'*. I realized this had to change. I also felt that I had done a lot for others but had failed to honor myself. It was not that I regretted having done things for others—it was more that I regretted not including myself in that process. I promised myself this would change.

Soon enough my own 'Emancipation Day' arrived. I said my goodbyes and made my way home to await the results of my final tests. It took quite some time. Three months passed before my oncologist advised me that I was in remission.

Obviously, I was relieved. April and I celebrated.

However, I did not bounce back the way I felt I should have. I know my body fairly well, and it seemed not to be responding to my newly-diagnosed healthy state. I checked with the doctors but they suggested that I give it more time; that recovery can be a slow process.

Slightly more than a year after my treatments had ended, I went to a local naturopath in Whitehorse where I was now living. I told her what I had been through and what I was currently experiencing. She gave me some supplements to help with the aftermath of cancer treatments. These tablets made the side of my neck swell up to a large size so I decided on my own to discontinue them.

At my next appointment I asked her why that happened. She was unsure and said she would research it for me. About a month later she had been unable to discover anything about this side effect and simply suggested a different kind of supplement. I tried them only to have the same result—my neck swelled up again.

Curious, I asked whether that might be because the supplements had detected cancer cells and were trying to fight them instead of simply helping me to recover from the treatments. She thought that might be a possibility, so I immediately booked an appointment with my family doctor. One look at my neck, and knowing my medical history, she immediately scheduled another series of cancer tests for me. I was back in the hospital having blood work, x-rays, ultrasound and, of course, the infamous CT scan.

Again, the waiting game.

Hoping against hope that the results would show me to be cancer-free, I waited for the call. The response was fairly quick this time, a matter of weeks.

The call came. Not only had the non-Hodgkin's Lymphoma returned but another cancer had been detected: Hodgkin's Lymphoma, both in my neck. My oncologist told me not to worry. Hodgkin's Lymphoma was better than Non-Hodgkin's, and he set up chemotherapy treatments right away. I advised him that I wanted some time to think about it first and consider other options.

In spite of my delay tactics, I received a call from the cancer centre in the Whitehorse General Hospital a week or so later wanting to schedule my treatments. When I advised the nurse that I wanted to explore other options, she enquired as to what those might be.

When I asked why, she seem concerned, and she responded, 'Did you know that Hodgkin's Lymphoma, if left untreated, is fatal?' I was shocked, as my oncologist had not seen fit to share that particular fact with me. Suddenly, I did not have the time I had thought to pursue naturopathic avenues of treatment. 'Fatal' was not something I wanted to mess with.

Once again, I was face to face with cancer.

However, in spite of the attention-grabbing 'fatal' aspect, the prognosis for Hodgkin's Lymphoma is quite good with a survival percentage in the 80 to 90 percent range. I was not dreading the chemotherapy, but was not doing cartwheels about it either. Somewhat reluctantly, I agreed to start the treatments right away.

Fortunately, the Whitehorse General Hospital is set up to administer chemotherapy, so I was spared the ordeal of having to fly south to a major centre for the treatments. I began the four-month regimen of chemo treatments, one every two weeks. I had foolishly thought at the beginning; 'Once every two weeks—how hard can that be?' My radiation treatments had been daily, so I figured that this shouldn't be too tough. That line of thinking came to an abrupt end with the first treatment.

I experienced every one of the possible side effects I was warned about, and some they didn't—the latter including hiccoughs, the extended play version, and an accelerated heart rate that lasted days at a time.

I had chosen to make my battle with cancer more widely known this time, primarily for the reason that I was working in an office in Whitehorse. Being a small town, word travels quickly, and I assumed that once my hair started falling out (more quickly than my advancing years was causing) people would figure it out. Letting people know turned out to be the very best thing I could have done.

The more difficult part was letting my children know. They had been quite worried the first time around and I was not looking forward to telling them I was having a second series of cancer treatments. I needn't have worried so much as they are great kids. Darren even offered to move north and look after me—a sincere and much appreciated offer.

I was, in fact, overwhelmed by the amount of support I was to receive. Aside from Darren, a number of other people offered to move in with me and help me out during the course of my treatments. I chose not to accept any of these generous and loving offers and I was grateful for the compassion behind them.

I am also blessed with many great friends in Whitehorse and they were incredibly supportive. At first, I found this difficult to accept, and I had to figure out why that was. Turns out I like to be the one doing the giving and not so much the one accepting.

Learning from my first experience with cancer, I meditated about this, and the answer I got was twofold:

1. *It is time to let go of the resistance and allow yourself to accept good things into your life (it ties in well with the concept of honoring myself) and,*

2. *Other people do care and want to help – so why would I want to deny them that opportunity?*

Needless to say, I chose to accept the support, and as it turns out it was a wise decision. On my worst days, when white cell counts were extremely low and it was not healthy for me to be out in public, friends would shop for me. They would leave the grocery bags on my doorstep, and ring the bell, staying a safe distance away so as not to run the risk of spreading their germs. Other friends cooked meals in for me; soup was much appreciated on days when my tongue and throat were swollen and sore.

People at work who I had not known that well offered to help me get through this ordeal. I was blown away by all this kind support. It showed me, up close and personal, people are at the core of their beings amazing and compassionate. It brought me to tears. My older brother (the one compiling this book) called me regularly to check in on me, giving me what loving support he could from a couple of thousand miles away. This was a huge gift, as he and I have never had a close relationship up until this point. It was an unexpected and much appreciated silver lining. A second gift was my sons helping me learn about the world of texting, and we stayed in touch frequently through that medium.

Not to say that the experience was all New Age Love and Enlightenment— not by a long shot. There were days when the pain was extremely intense, and the Cancer Clinic only wanted me to take acetaminophen so as not to interfere with what the chemo was doing. I both understood and supported their reasoning intellectually. However, on a purely physical level, it was an entirely different matter. The acetaminophen did absolutely nothing for my pain.

It felt as though all my joints were on fire. I could not sleep; I was unable to find a pain-free position. I tried every piece of furniture in the house, and even the floor, but nothing supported my quest for sleep! Some days my painful sleeplessness was combined with pain and swelling in my throat and tongue so much so that I could barely swallow even soft things. I just wanted to curl up in a ball and die.

I tried to focus on the big picture and remind myself that this was a temporary period that would end soon enough, and that I would, in all likelihood, recover. By the end of each two-week period, I would inevitably start to feel better and be 'ready' just in time to start the cycle of chemo.

I went to work as often as I could. I do like my job and the great people there. It was also therapeutic; being at work, and focusing on tasks there took my mind off my personal situation for a while.

Was chemotherapy a challenging experience to go through? Absolutely. Did my potential death force me to the wall? Undoubtedly. Am I going to tell you that I came close to death, saw the light and my late sister, Jody? No. But I came very close.

My experience with cancer showed me that both life and people are very special, and that I will never know when either could be taken from me. I am resolved to do my best to enjoy and appreciate my own life, my family, and friends. I made new friends and new discoveries about myself, both helping my life be more fulfilling and joyful than it was.

Am I out of the woods? No. The Hodgkin's Lymphoma is in remission, but the non-Hodgkin's Lymphoma is still with me. It is not widespread and will be monitored regularly. To me this is fairly minor in the grand scheme of things.

What's next? Well, truth be told, I kinda like my brother's new 'motto' in his career as what I am calling a 'Life and Death Coach'
Create a Life Worth Dying For and a Death Worth Living
ForI am going to get started on just that!"

MARTA'S STORY

I was talking with a friend of mine today about death and dying. Marta and I were exploring the possibility of her writing about how her culture in Costa Rica deals with death. All of a sudden she was overcome by emotions and memories of her brother's death of some thirty years ago. I asked her to tell me what was going on for her.

"I don't know where to begin, Stephen. My skin is crawling and I want to get out of my body. I just want to go back to bed and sleep forever and not ever have to deal with this pain again, although in a way that is exactly what I've been doing for thirty years, pushing things down, just going through the motions of life. In a way it's like a part of me went into that casket with my brother and never escaped. Sometimes, often, I feel like am still there with him," Marta replied.

"Can you tell me something about your brother's death?" I asked.

"I was six years old when Eduardo got sick—six years old! He was my brother, my buddy, my protector. He was eight. We used to do everything together, play, pull pranks on people, laugh and just live life as children." Marta paused and seemed very uncomfortable. She carried on:

"I'm thinking again, its safer for me this way—I would rather think through this. I really don't want to feel any of this! Why the hell did you ask me to do this, Stephen? I don't know how to say all that I feel! I don't know how to be mad! What do you want me to say?"

Marta was emotional and full of anger, almost rage. Then she exploded.

"WHY DID YOU TAKE HIM FROM ME? WHY? WHAT WAS THE REASON FOR KILLING HIM LIKE THAT?" she sobbed angrily. "He suffered so much—what kind of bastard is a God who would let this happen? What kind of nasty life is this?" Marta wondered.

"I've just never got it. He was a child, a good child, smart, sweet, always thinking of others and so very kind. He was brave, always trying to protect Mom and us girls! And you, God, systematically mutilated him. Not only did he have to go through the devastation of losing his leg, but then chemo and radiation and getting his entire right lung removed. Then there was nothing else that could be done." Marta cried deeply, feeling the pain her brother must have felt as he struggled daily with cancer.

Continuing, she said, "Only morphine every eight hours would ease the pain. Then, every seven hours, every six, five, four, three, two, and one hour. By the time he died he was getting injections every half hour! He was always in devastating pain. He looked like a living skeleton; he couldn't eat, or talk, let alone play."

More tears and sorrow gushed from her heart.

"Here is the weird thing about this nightmare", she said. "I was angry at him, so damn angry for abandoning me. He left me all alone with cold parents and no love. There was no one who seemed to care about anything, especially about me. All that mattered was that Eduardo was dead. Everyone was angry, and it felt like they were angry at me." She paused again to catch her breath, and then continued on.

"We didn't handle it well in my family; Mom just cried and ate. Dad went out dancing and drinking with his buddies. All I could think of was Eduardo; he had just died a thousand deaths every day for two long painful years! Who allows this, who enabled it to happen? Why would God let this go on in the life of such an innocent sweet child?" Marta continued to express her deepest and long held pain.

"Then he died," she said, rather stone faced.

"Mom says he 'goes to rest with the angels'. She's not crying but Dad, well, he is crying for all of us. I'm not crying either—I'm just cold inside and out. Always cold! People come and go in and out of the shack where we live looking busy and concerned, but no one looks at me. No one talks to me. I just walk around aimlessly. I have nowhere to go. I just sit there staring into space wondering when this agony will end."

We sat quietly for a few moments, and then Marta continued to paint the picture of the pain and desperation she felt as a young child witnessing the challenging death of her dear brother.

"I remember people praying furiously for Eduardo's sou—for *all* of our souls so we can 'accept the will of God'. They all wanted to help us pray to God, but it felt to me that no one really saw me or my family. No one wanted to see us; they were just happy that it was not their kid that God took apart in little pieces."

She went on to say, "The only help I got was from my grandpa who sat by me mumbling prayers. He'd been sitting there forever, it seemed, and then he finally reached over and hugged me. YES ME! I cried a little, and felt the warmth of grandpa's hug run through my body. I just want to feel that warm a little longer, and prayed, 'Please God, let him hold me a little longer!' But just like that it was over, and I dropped back to my cold and alone limbo."

"The rest of the ordeal was more like a carnival than anything else," Marta related. "People screaming, my dad wailing like a school girl, and mom saying it's because he feels guilty. She doesn't feel guilty at all, though, as she did her duty, so she doesn't need to cry like that. My aunties are mad at her, saying, 'she must not have loved Eduardo at all, that bitch!' and then they cry a little louder."

She remembers, "There were thousands of people walking with us to the cemetery, one of the biggest funeral processions ever seen in town—all because Eduardo was such a good kid and everybody loved him. I've never seen most of these people in my life! Yet they all pile up and around, pushing to get a glimpse of Eduardo or the family of the celebrity. They stare, trying to figure it all out I think. All of a sudden we are there at the cement box where Eduardo will disappear forever. Now the real circus begins. People screaming everywhere, some faint, some throw themselves at the casket. I just stand back and watch it all happen, cold as hell. I remember shaking like a rabbit, just watching, my brain frozen. Dad's calling me to look at Eduardo 'one last time'.

I can't feel anything—I just continue to shiver and shake. I don't know if I even looked at his face one last time or not. I just remember the concrete lid slamming shut in the distance like a sledge hammer was hitting my head, and the screeching of that little metal spatula they use to mix the fresh concrete that they will use to seal the cement box with Eduardo inside. I was cold, alone and in limbo."

I found myself wondering if Marta ever really completed her journey of grief for her dear brother Eduardo. It seemed to me like it was still stuck in her adult body, mind, and heart. So I asked her about it, and this is what she said:

"You see, even now I feel numb and unattached from everything and everyone—alone and in limbo. Whenever life is too much, I just go there. I freeze and stop feeling, even though I know now why this is. The shock and trauma were too much for me when I was little, and I had no one in my life to help me through it all. I just lived with the horrifying memories of Eduardo's fight with cancer and his death. It became a habit and how I dealt with change and loss as an adult."

"I was really angry at God, as none of my brother's suffering and his death made sense to me. I blamed God for it all and walked away from 'His' churches and religions altogether. I decided that when you are 'loyal' to God, bad things happen to you and your family, so instead I feel dead inside, poisoned, more lost than I ever thought possible!" Marta paused and caught her breath, then continued. "Truth is I would rather a million times feel rage than this apathetic numbness in my soul—this numbness creeps into everything in my life. I'm so tired of living this way! I really have nothing left to say. I am just empty, bitter and sad—a numbing cold all over my body except for my throat—that is the only place that burns."

Marta's story soulfully illustrates what happens when grief gets pushed away, ignored or mishandled. I am deeply grateful for her willingness to bare her soul for all to see in order that others learn to handle grief with even more love acceptance and compassion.

Destroying is a necessary function in life. Everything has its season, and all things eventually lose their effectiveness and die.—Margaret J. Wheatley

CHAPTER FIVE

Unexpected Death, Suicide and
Abortion—A Silent Struggle

Sorrow that is never spoken is the heaviest load to bear.—Frances Ridley Havergal

© 2009 barbara cameron pix

THERE IS NO SHAME IN YOUR DESOLATION

Sudden, unexpected death and suicide are two deaths that can be the most difficult to deal with. This is not to diminish the impact of other deaths, but more to identify the unique reactions the survivors have to face. If death is taboo, then sudden death, especially suicide, is extremely so. Because of the stigma of sudden death, survivors are often faced with silence and dealing with the death on their own or in a small family unit.

In this chapter, I want to shine some light on these challenges and the unique reactions survivors can experience. Many take sudden death or suicide very personally. They may assume more blame and guilt, often feeling extremely hopeless and very angry. Suicide survivors can take these feelings to the extreme. On some level the survivors feel they should have done something to prevent the tragic event.

I have known two families who lost loved ones to suicide: one was a father, and the other a son. The reactions were extreme, and the grief journey was significantly longer and much more volatile. The emotions seemed to be magnified, especially the anger and guilt. Some of these reactions were caused by the double hit not only of the death but the fact that it was unexpected, and by suicide.

One of the most significant challenges, though, is the self-imposed silence of the survivors, and their unwillingness to talk about it. Additionally, there is the trauma a survivor feels when they recognize that a loved one has left them this way. They didn't leave by divorce, or by walking out or any more 'normal' ways of leaving. The survivors also feel betrayed that their loved one wouldn't allow them to help.

The result of this cone of silence is that the surviving family and friends are often unable to grieve fully. That journey is suspended or frozen in time. Often grief is halted for many, many years. The natural flow of grief is locked up inside as a direct result of the taboo placed by our culture on suicide and sudden death. Suicide is somehow linked to homicide, and both are dreaded topics of conversation.

Another aspect that the family needs to cope with is the reaction of friends, co-workers and acquaintances viewing the death from the outside. There is a tendency in sudden deaths, especially suicide, to be labeled insane, evil, or shameful. These beliefs are often placed on the survivors, too.

I had a great conversation with a dear friend of mine the other day. Jen and I were having dinner at my favorite Thai restaurant, catching up with each other. Her father committed suicide a year ago, so the topic of course came up. I asked her if it would be alright if I wrote of our chat in my book and she said, "Absolutely."

I asked Jen what she wanted others to know about her Dad's suicide. What gems of wisdom could she pass along to people?

"I tried forever to understand why Dad killed himself. I did my best to make sense out of it all," she said. " But I couldn't—it just didn't add up for me. The only way I could have had any hope of understanding is to have lived his fifty-four years of life, and yet even then I likely wouldn't have understood. The reality is that Dad likely didn't even understand." Jen paused for a moment and then continued: "Let's be clear: if my Dad felt inside him that there was any other option than death, he would have taken that option for sure, but obviously he had gotten to a place where there was no other option for him. That is the part I can never understand."

We sat quietly for a few moments. I asked her if there were other things she wanted to share.

"I thought about all the plans I had with Dad. Vacations together, buying an RV, and building an addition on the home. I was remembering all the great times we shared together and our amazing relationship." Jen went on to say, "And I almost threw all of that away because, if life was that good, why would he have killed himself? It was crazy-making!" She spoke again: "What was crazy was the death is that our life together was great. I am so glad I didn't throw the baby out with the bath water. What I want people to know is that when I finally accepted the fact that I could never understand why, I was able to let go of having to know, and to allow myself to feel the loss. That acceptance really helped me to move along my path of grief and begin to heal."

We had a few more bites of dinner, and sat quietly again for a moment or two. I checked in again, asking if there was anything else she wanted you all to know.

"Although it was really traumatic for me at the time, seeing my Dad's body where he killed himself was really important," she said quietly. "His body was cold and lifeless. When I touched him, I knew in an instant that he wasn't there in his body. It was shocking and really hard to witness, and yet seeing him lying there dead was an anchor for me. The visual scene made it real—there was no denying it. Dad was dead."

"You know, it was really intense—the morgue, the funeral, all the phones calls, the lawyers, all the arrangements and logistics. Stephen, it was unreal. I got caught up in all of that, and every time some grief popped up I pushed it aside and dealt with the details instead. I know now that grief has its own way and its own time schedule. What I want people to know is to put the details second. Be compassionate, patient, and gentle with yourself; when emotions come up, put them first. The details will get taken care of."

I asked her, "What did people do that was really helpful?"

"The most helpful thing people did was to send cards," Jen said, sounding a little surprised at her own answer. "It was so crazy busy after Dad's death, and there was so much to do that I wasn't able to really pay attention to what people were saying to me. Though I did my best to listen, I really didn't hear much. The cards though, they were great. I could read them on my own schedule and I could read them over and over again. The cards were very comforting."

Without even taking a breath, Jen continued: "When people took care of logistics and getting details handled, that really helped. Especially when people took care of meals and cleaning up after." She smiled and completed with, "And they could have continued with the meal thing way longer!"

We took a pause for tea and food and then continued on.

"When people put music on I found it very healing. Sometimes there would be a song that reminded me of Dad and I would cry. Other times the song would have me dancing and moving, it was all good. Yes, play music! It soothed my aching soul," She said with a smile.

"Oh, and my friend Tina, boy did she help out!" Curious at Jen's exuberance, I nodded encouraging her to carry on. "Yes, Tina just sat and listened; she didn't try to fix anything or change anything. She just listened and held me."

Jen continued: "James did that too. I remember one time I was just so sad and crying so hard. He came over to me and held me close. Didn't say a word. He just held me snugly and let me cry until I was done. That was so helpful. No words—just being there was way more than enough. Oh, and taking care of our kids, so James and I could have some time together in the storm of all the busy, crazy times was awesome!"

Without skipping a beat she said, "Now here are some things that *didn't* work for me. Don't make promises and then not keep them. I was so busy and so overwhelmed that I really did need the help. I needed help—not just a promise. I know that people meant well, but broken promises at that time really hurt."

Appreciating her approach, I asked her to continue with what didn't work.

"When people tried to fix it or make me feel better somehow, it really didn't work for me at all. My grief had a mind of its own, and a time schedule unique to me. I wasn't broken and didn't need to be fixed. I just needed to be heard. Advice wasn't helpful either, nor were comparisons."

Jen remembered a time when someone with the best of intentions said that she knew how Jen must have felt. Though Jen bit her tongue she remembered thinking, "You have *no* idea how I feel, and don't assume that you do."

I felt her anger and hurt, so I asked about it.

"Look," she said firmly, " My journey along my *own* grief path is mine, and it is unique to me. Yes, others may have had a similar experience, and I get they want me to know they understand or feel for me. But they don't, and can't, so please don't assume you do." She completed with, "It's much better to be quiet and listen."

Continuing, Jen said to me, "I really understand now how important it is to support others in their own unique way of grieving, to find ways to make their process of grief 'right'. Expression like 'This too will pass' bothered me as it felt like the one saying that to me wanted me to get on with my life and that my grief process was in some way wrong."

After another pause, I asked her what she would do differently.

"Well, I would take the time to say to Dad what I wanted to say to him. I got so carried away with the details of the ceremony and other people's needs. I tried my best to do the politically correct things, and as a result I left myself out."

She went right on to say, "I would also make sure that I gathered around me my heart peeps (people)—friends and family that I know really get me. My grief needs to be received too. I am actually planning a second ceremony of my Dad's death, and will take the time say all those things I needed to say but left out for one reason or another."

I asked Jen next what she had learned about life through the experience of her father's death.

"I learned to make time for the important things in life. Family, friends, sharing time together really. I want to create memories for my own family! I also learned how important James, my husband, is to me, and that I want to have more quality time with him to deepen our relationship. Experiencing death this way has taught me so much about appreciating life each day."

Jen closed our conversation by saying; "It is so good to talk about it all; it makes it real when I get in touch with how I feel. Truth is, my Dad is not those ashes in a box. I can feel him around me when I take the time to reconnect with what I know to be him. What was living in him is still with me every day."

Thanks Jen, I appreciate you sharing so openly with us.

Another friend, Reuben WeinStangel, has studied suicide extensively and researched its impact on family and friends. When I asked Reuben to send along some of his findings he was really happy to do so. His writing sheds some compassionate light on one of the most difficult deaths for survivors to cope with. I have included his entire piece in the "Additional Resources" section of the book so that those of you who have experienced this type of loss can dive more deeply into the topic.

Here are some highlights from Reuben's compassionate and sensitive contribution to my book. Thank you Reuben!

THE STORY OF ROBERT

Robert was a successful businessman with a wife and three children. He was in his mid-fifties, had a large social support network, and had no previously diagnosed cases of mental illness in his medical history. His friends and family described him as a kind-hearted and thoughtful person, but the extent of these qualities were not fully appreciated until after he had already killed himself.

As he explained it, suicide was a strong desire of his since he was eleven years old. Although he came from a loving household, and had good friends at school, he always felt like he was living his life from the outside looking in. He never felt like he belonged or that he connected to this world in any meaningful way. Years later, this feeling festered in his marriage and family life. A sense of detachment from his life developed and a feeling of dissatisfaction grew with it.

What makes Robert a special case is that he took well over a year of planning before he successfully followed through with his decision. Every member of his family was considered, as were his close friends, and the people with whom he worked. He spent his time making sure that all loose ends were tied up and that each person he cared about would be taken care of when he was gone.

He left behind a neatly typed package divided into categories for each person in his life. There was a personalized note for each person within, often several pages in length, explaining his decision and what he had done to make things more comfortable for them. His office work was completed three months in advance so that they would have time to interview his replacement. He made sure that all the financials for his family were taken care of for several years to come. Everybody was left with a goodbye, a reminder of how much he loved them, and just how much they meant to him.

On his final day, he went to work, as usual. He came home that night, went to the basement, left the package in a visible place, and hung himself. He was discovered later that night when his family came home.

DISCUSSION

Oftentimes delaying the inevitable may be enough to have the person rethink their position. However, Robert took his time and kept this decision to himself. There was no indication of warning and, while we'd like to believe that anyone looking to kill themselves must be certifiably insane, it would seem that he reached this decision from a place of calm introspection.

Robert had a strong social support network, was financially secure, had no recorded history of mental illness, no familial history of suicide, and even appeared to be happy until his dying day. The choice was made independently and without coercion from external influences. He was not drunk or under the influence of any drugs at the time at the death. In fact, it appeared throughout the investigation as if he was in a sound mental state throughout the process.

All indications pointed to a long-standing existential crisis as the root cause of his chosen escape. He was overwhelmed by the enormity of his problem and saw suicide as a logical way out. He wrote that death was a welcome release and that he embraced it with open arms.

Robert's family expressed remorse at the fact that they never knew his subjective state of mind until it was too late. He felt alone and disconnected, even when he was surrounded by the people who loved him the most. His wife knew about his previous suicide attempt, but thought that it was a callous act of an impulsive adolescent. She thought that period in his life was long over and could not understand how he could have planned for so long without telling her how he felt.

He lived his life with the ongoing and continual consideration of suicide. As he described it, it was always in the back of his mind as a way out. Even with his explanations, it is difficult to say exactly what sparked his decision to die. Perhaps it was his pervasive contemplation on the subject led to the calm and methodical decision that he did not want to live anymore. His family and friends were considered at length, but even they were not enough of a reason to dissuade him from his choice.

His decision was not the result of an isolated and temporary set of circumstances. His reasons were not environmental or social in nature. Rather, his dissatisfaction came from an internal feeling of social segregation and exclusion. While others willingly accepted him in their lives, he never felt like he was one of them.

POST-THOUGHTS

One of the paradoxes of suicide is that it can seem as if it happens as the result of a single reason. The decision to die is not a random decision, but is actually the result of a build-up. There is an ever-present cycle of tormenting thoughts that the person experiences day-after-day. When a person is living in this spiraling state of mind, they experience a wearing away of their mental resistance. Risk factors begin to pile up, and stressors remain prevalent and unyielding in the individual's perception of events. Somewhere along this spectrum, a moment occurs when the threshold limit of tolerance is reached, and the scales may tip in favor of death.

However, just because a person is having difficulty in one area of their life now, doesn't mean they are incompetent in other areas of their life. Current problems do not indicate future or past issues. Minor positive changes act as catalysts to recovery. These victories can start to outweigh problematic circumstances as practical small steps lead to achievements. Achievements bolster self-esteem, resulting in a restored feeling of competence and self-worth. It is in seeing potential for long-term change that we feel a renewed sense of vitality towards our efforts. After a few minor victories, a steadfast resolve often develops where the person is not willing to settle for anything less than the total attainment of their goals. This improved state of self is vital to tipping the scales back in favor of life.

The ways in which we choose to see life has a powerful impact on our feelings of belonging and connection to the world. Our feelings of existential peace, happiness, and meaning are intricately tied to our environment, social world, and subjective internal states. Furthermore, how we choose to see death will shape how we decide to leave this world. It can be a beautiful departure or a horrific escape.

Suicide is a choice, but one that rarely comes as the result of a calm and introspective decision; rather, it is likely a reaction to a set of circumstances. Death is a final solution when a person believes that there is no other option. As a practical consideration, there is more potential to life than we could ever hope to realize. It should logically follow that all other alternatives should be explored first. Oftentimes, many of these options remain unexplored before it is too late.

Reuben thank you for your open and compassionate look at suicide.

ABORTION
THE PRIVATE AND INVISIBLE DEATHS

Another death that occurs and often gets pushed aside is abortion—the loss of a loved one yet to be born. Allison, a friend of mine, recently related the story of her choice to abort a pregnancy. She told me all the details of how she got pregnant, how she made the choice to abort, how the father reacted, and much more. It was a moving, interesting, and very personal look at this loss.

ALLISON'S STORY: THE RAINBOW OF DEATH

"Allison, tell me something about the guy you were involved with, and your relationship," I prompted.

"I always knew he wasn't the man I wanted to have a long-term relationship with," she said. "Yet for some weird reason there was something about unprotected sex with him that I let be acceptable. I wasn't on the pill, so I would always nudge him to remember a condom. He didn't. Next thing I knew, really to no one's surprise, my period was late."

"So what went through your mind when you realized your period was late?" I asked.

"I started to ask myself the big questions: *If I am pregnant, what am I going to do? Could I have a child right now? Do I want a child right now? Could I carry a child to term then put it up for adoption? What about having an abortion?*" Allison said.

She went on with the story: "Three weeks into lateness, I bought a home pregnancy test. It came out positive.

Three days later I went to the doctor to be tested just to be extra sure—again, the result was positive.

I was definitely pregnant," she said soberly.

Carrying on, she said, "When I told the baby's father, his instant reaction was that he didn't want it. And he was adamant. It was in that moment that I knew no matter what decision I made about the baby, I was alone on this journey. Despite the mental fear, I started to get excited. Internally, bodily, and emotionally, I realized that I wanted the baby."

"So what did you do next?" I asked.

Allison continued: "Though I was terrified, I decided to tell my parents. I knew they loved being grandparents to my nephew, but my situation was so different than my married brother's. I had no idea how they would react. I remember it was a Wednesday night. I got them both on the phone at the same time and asked, 'So, how would you like to be grandparents again?' Thankfully, all I felt radiating through the phone was pure love, joy, excitement, and a willingness to support me however they could. I was so relieved!"

"So what happened to change your mind?" I asked.

"A week or so later I noticed things inside me started to shift. The reality of keeping the baby set in; the financial, emotional, and spiritual implications of raising a child alone brought me back down to earth pretty quickly. But how could I have an abortion? Could I consciously choose to terminate a pregnancy? What would people say and think if they found out? I thought, *I'm not eighteen anymore; I'm a grown-up, so I should be able to do this. How would I live with myself if I terminated my pregnancy? What the hell am I supposed to do?* All these questions raced through my head I felt scared, confused, and really didn't know what to do."

She sat quietly as if remembering the exact moment, and then carried on:

"I went back to my doctor and asked her about my options. We talked about abortion and parenting and she asked me some really good questions about how I envisioned my life and my child's life. I sought counsel from an energy healer I have been with for the last six years. I also got firsthand accounts from a friend who has been through a pregnancy termination."

"After gathering all this information, I found myself laying awake many nights for hours, tossing and turning, staring up at the ceiling, meditating and praying, dreaming and trusting the right decision would come through at the perfect moment. Finally one night, eight weeks into the pregnancy, the inner battle subsided and I came to terms with my decision, the decision I always knew I was going to make. In that moment of clarity I emailed the clinic to request an appointment for the abortion; two days later the confirmation arrived." A few tears trickled down her face as she sat still in the memory of her decision.

"Once you made the decision what was it like for you?: I asked.

"I was scared, not just about what it would be like after the pregnancy was terminated, but that people would find out I was pregnant. What would they say? What would they think of me? What would I tell them after the pregnancy was terminated? I didn't want people to know I was pregnant then have to turn around and tell them there was no more baby. I struggled with who to tell and how much of the truth I wanted to share. I was awash with understanding the intimate nature of my decision to terminate the pregnancy, and wanting to be open about what was going on. It was hard. In the end, I decided to tell only my immediate family and a few of my closest friends," Allison related with a big sigh.

"Tell me about the day of the abortion," I said.

"Well, I woke up early, showered and put on my most comforting clothes— the bottoms of a set of scrubs that belonged to my Pépère, my grandfather, as they reminded me he was always with me, a man-sized t-shirt of the softest cotton that felt like a big protective hug, and my Zumba hoodie because it just felt good. My friend picked me up and we drove to the clinic."

Allison's voice cracked a little as she continued. "I was greeted respectfully by the medical staff, and felt as comfortable as I could in such an uncomfortable situation. I looked around the waiting room at the other women—some with girl friends and some with their boyfriends. My heart went out to the women and couples who were agonizing over their decision, knowing there was no chance for a do-over. My girl friend and I talked about everyday things, as we normally would any other time, sometimes laughing too loudly, sometimes getting lost in our own thoughts, sometimes locking eyes with a deep knowing, understanding, and compassion. I joked with the ultrasound technician about the cruelty of making a pregnant woman fast for so long. I shared with the counselor how my grieving had already begun."

"My turn arrived. I was taken to a second waiting room, instructed to change, and given some Ativan to help me relax. The TV was on the infomercial channel. I sat staring, breathing, riding the waves of emotion that were coursing through my heart. I talked to the unborn child inside me—'Little Man' as I had affectionately named him. I prayed for strength and courage to make it through with ease and grace."

She sat still for a moment, remembering the events as if it just happened yesterday.

"A second nurse arrived and took me to the procedure room. She was petite with long blonde hair. I remember her loving, compassionate, tender energy. As she put the intravenous needle in my arm we made small talk about how long she'd been a nurse and why she chose to continue to work in the clinic. I wish I remembered her answer.

"The doctor came in; they put more drugs into my IV. They started the machines, put the mask on my face, and told me to breath deeply. There was a big twinge. I took bigger and deeper breaths, and then it was done."

"Empty. Baby was gone. Instantly, I started to cry."

"They said I did great and wondered if I was in any pain. 'None physically,' I said, and in less than five minutes I was sitting in a recovery room, with a heating pad on my abdomen, sipping Canada Dry, and eating cookies. My friend came in. We cried together."

Allison took a deep breath and carried on.

"The recovery nurse gave me my package of post-care instructions and a prescription for antibiotics, and we were on our way home. On the way out I stopped—I was taken aback as I glanced around the waiting room—there wasn't an empty seat to be found. I was shocked at how widespread the decision to have an abortion really was."

Allison spoke about her recovery.

"The physical healing process was smooth and effortless. I feel lucky. I walked a little bit everyday, even if it was only from one end of my apartment to the other. I ate healthy food to maintain my energy. I rested a lot. Though I still felt like I was living in a foggy dream, my life slowly got back to normal—the minutes, days, weeks, and months have passed by. The absence of the baby in my belly makes it all feel like some kind of dream," she reflected.

"My greatest struggle has been to remember the whole event and honor the grief that has, at times, been paralyzing. I mourn the loss of my dream of starting my own family that I always thought would make me somehow feel more complete. The grief shifted from being solely about the baby and the abortion, to the loss of all the aspects of being a mom: breastfeeding, decorating a nursery, sleepless nights, and all those newborn sounds and smells, to the loss of the dream."

Allison, noticeably upset, continued: "The emptiness in my uterus and the ache in my heart has been unbearable at times. There are still periods of extreme heartache, supreme anger, rage at the baby's father, emptiness that seems to have no end, guilt for killing my baby, and frustration that I still find myself dipping back into this pit of darkness."

Before I could ask, she spoke, "Thankfully, to the depth I felt darkness and despair, I have developed a greater capacity to feel love and joy—what a gift! I also have a deeper understanding of myself, and my values. There is a lot more love flowing through my heart for myself and others that I never knew existed before. The love and joy continues to pour through me in my relationships with friends, family, coworkers, and with complete strangers walking down the street." Allison beamed. "I laugh harder, I love more deeply, I have more gratitude for the simple things. I feel more peaceful, and I live with greater clarity."

In wrapping up her story, she shared, "While this experience has been the most difficult of my life, the wins have been profound. I have realized there are many people who love me and who will support me. I have learned that it's up to me to ask for support—it's not a sign of weakness, but a sign of strength that I choose to be authentic and vulnerable, and let the depth of all of my emotions be felt and seen by myself and others. I would never have planned this whole journey, yet in my heart I am grateful for the lessons that have changed my life forever."

Thank you Allison for sharing such an intimate and private piece of your life.

Suicide has a profound, traumatic effect upon individuals left behind, one that is still not entirely recognized by the medical community or the public. Family members and other loved ones feel isolated by the suicidal act and its aftermath. —Christopher Lukas

CHAPTER SIX

Embracing Death—A Survivor's Manual

The idea of death, the fear of it, haunts the human animal like nothing else; it is a mainspring of human activity – designed largely to avoid the fatality of death, to overcome it by denying in some way that it is the final destiny of man. —Ernest Becker

OPENING THE DOOR

Death is tucked right over your shoulder, lurking in the background where we try to keep it hidden. Maintaining our distance seems comfortable, giving us 'permission' to avoid it altogether.

The opposite of death is, of course, birth. Can you imagine giving a newborn baby distance, avoiding them like they have the plague? Why then do we do this at an equally intimate time called death, at a time when the one dying needs our heart's presence more than we can imagine? We are 'taught' to pull back into supposed safety. That being said, whether we keep our distance or not, we are absolutely in the energetic field of the dying person! By our very proximity to them we pick up all manner of conscious and subconscious 'stuff' not even noticing it until one day we break down, feel stuck, want to quit, or simply build even thicker walls to protect ourselves from all of this death fallout.

What is even more impactful is that you are not only living with the one dying, you are also involved with your entire family and each of their own issues regarding death! No wonder you may be feeling overwhelmed, tired to the core, and uncertain as to how to manage in the sea of chaos and change that often surrounds death.

The result of you and your family's contact with death affects everyone. Recent studies done by Raising the Bar staff researchers indicate that an average five to eight people around a death are significantly affected by the loss of a loved one. Death really stirs things up! This includes our children.

© 2011 barbara cameron pix

SOAR ABOVE THE NORM. FREE YOURSELF FROM THE HABIT OF SILENCE

OUR CHILDREN

As adults, it is our responsibility to teach children—our own and others—how to deal with the loss of a loved one. Showing them how to be open, honest, and loving while experiencing a painful loss will help young ones learn about both the joy and the pain that results from loving family and friends deeply. It will help them embrace fully both life and death.

Although much of what is written in the body of this section applies to children, there are unique considerations we need to make for our young ones. There is information regarding how children grieve that applies specifically to them, and information that will help adults support a process that is distinct from adult grief.

I have included a mini manual on this topic that is included in the "Additional Resources Section" at the end of this book. Such an important topic deserves special attention!

New ways of dealing with death and its impact on you, your family, and friends are needed if in fact we are to survive—and more importantly, *thrive*—in this era of increasing numbers of deaths being brought to us by the huge baby boomer generation, the media, and its constant reporting of war and catastrophe. Here are some *guiding phrases* you can use to help change your approach to death, phrases that will also help you teach others new ways to embrace death:

- Talk about death open-heartedly

- Learn to accept the reality of the loss
- Get and stay involved with family and friends
- Practice gentleness, kindness, and compassion
- Enjoy what life you have left as fully as you can
- Create a support system for yourself
- Talk about and plan the way you want to die

CREATING A TOOL BOX

We need to re-train ourselves to live with death and the process of death in deeper and healthier ways that includes all the hidden opportunities death affords. This is hard to practice when it only comes around occasionally in our families. However, there are other traumatic times that occur regularly in life that can teach us how to deal with the inevitable loss of a loved one, and for that matter, our own future death.

Here are some other types of 'death' that we can practice with in order to learn some closure skills that will stand us in good stead:

- Fired or retired from a job
- End of a relationship
- Completion of a project
- End of a day
- Depletion of your bank account
- Death of a dream
- Death of an age or era
- Loss of a faculty (sight, hearing, etc.)

When thinking of death we tend to focus on a person's passing or loss of the body. Agreed, this is the big one, and yet we can prepare for this by understanding that these other 'deaths' are similar experiences. Something existed and now it no longer does. Let's take a look at some of the other 'deaths' listed above and see how we can use them to practice acceptance, closure, and letting go.

The ending of a *relationship* is a great comparison, as many, if not all of us, have ended a loving relationship at one time or another. If you were the one who was left it can feel devastating for quite a time after. The roller-coaster ride of emotions can be very similar to the emotional ride described earlier on. This is particularly true of long-standing relationships.

You will notice, especially immediately after the breakup, that your emotions can get easily triggered when you see your ex-partner, or when you visit the home of a mutual friend. You may notice the loss when you walk by a favorite restaurant or when a special occasion comes and goes. You may notice those feelings of trying to get him or her back—bargaining—and perhaps even denial ("Oh, they'll come to their senses and we'll get back together!"). This mini-death mimics quite closely the demise of life.

We can use the ending of an important relationship to practice the skills of *acknowledging* the loss, *accepting* the benefits, *saying good-bye* well, and *being real* with our deepest feelings. We can also practice the use of *ceremony or ritual* to mark in a healthy way the end of this important piece of our lives. Notice how you reacted when ending a relationship. What did you do well? What could you improve upon? What skills, tools, and techniques did you learn that you could use when facing the death of a loved one or other life endings? When you practice this process, you will build yourself a 'Death Toolbox' that you can draw on when needed.

Death, or the ending of a *job* can be equally tough on people, especially when the job loss was unexpected or sudden. Many of the same emotions similar to ending a relationship will arise as you move through the process of job loss or job change. You will feel denial, bargaining, and anger, sadness, and often confusion occurring regularly and sometimes forcefully as you move from employed to unemployed. Even if the job change was planned as in the case of retirement, there will still be a journey through grief as you adjust to the change and different environment and the loss of personal worth and business relationships.

You may notice that even when you find another job you are still carrying mental and emotional baggage from the exit of your previous job. You may find yourself wishing you were back in your old position and remembering 'better' days. On the other side of the coin, you may carry the emotional and mental baggage with relief ("Whew, glad *that's* over"), yet you are still lugging it along as you compare one job to the other.

At some point it's done, and you are in your new position with no hang-over from the previous one. So again, notice how you approach this death. What did you do well that supported that change? What did you do that didn't really work that well? What pitfalls did you stumble into and get stuck in for a while? Add the tools that worked for you to your Death Toolbox and do some research on where you may have gotten stuck or lost.

Here is a really simple one:

Each day is born as we awaken to the new morning. Each day dies into the darkness of night as we fall asleep. There is death and rebirth each and every day! It's a time to say good-bye to what is no longer, and a time to greet that which is new. What a wonderful practice! Do you have a way to begin each day aside from simply getting out of bed? Do you have a way to close each day so it doesn't unwillingly force itself into tomorrow? Do you have tools to notice what you did well that day and celebrate those wins? Do you have ways to let go of what you didn't do so well and forgive yourself?

Add these simple easy-to-practice skills and tools to your Death Toolbox and help yourself prepare for the unavoidable deaths that will come your way.

Look at all the different types of death that remain on the list, and discover how you can 'practice' all of the skills that you can then transfer and use when the death of a loved one comes knocking on your door.

Hey, even in sex there is birth and death! Birth of sexual play begins with the urge. It comes alive and blossoms into lovemaking and at the end of the sexual encounter there is the *petit mort* (which means "little death") in the form of an orgasm. The sexual encounter has completed itself and has died.

So, notice these opportunities to gratefully let go of the old and to embrace that which is new.

Along with these practice opportunities it would also be helpful to have some reliable skills and practical tools that you can count on to help you, your family, and friends. These skills will support you in dealing with the staff and volunteers within the professional health care system. The more tools you have, the more skilled you will be at communicating and navigating the turbulent seas of death and change—for both yourself and your family.

So let's continue with the building of your toolbox.

Having an understanding of death and the journey of grief and loss is fantastic. This knowledge will support you when dealing with both the person dying and the family members and friends remaining. This knowledge is much like a road map that you can use to locate where you and others are in the process. Though you may be overwhelmed with the emotions of the moment, this knowledge will at least allay the feeling of being lost at sea in it all.

The previous chapters set some great groundwork for you to stand on, and broadened your understanding of death from many different perspectives. I hope they helped you look at death a little differently so when you face it you may not be so startled. The real-life stories others shared helped you experience dying indirectly through someone else's eyes, ears, and hearts.

With all this foundational work done, we can now add the practical part: talking to each other! This may not be as easy as it seems—most people are in the death denial camp. They haven't the necessary skill set to handle these often-challenging conversations, This is why we have trained professionals and hospice volunteers!

So lets get these hospice skills into your own hands!

We will begin with basic communication skills and then add emotional management, some questioning techniques and finally some small group facilitation practices. You will be able to support your family and friends in talking with each other respectfully, lovingly, and compassionately.

The goal of communication, by the way, is to create mutual understanding by speaking, writing, or using signs. We communicate primarily by using words, by using our body in the form of gestures, facial expressions, breathing and touch, and by the tone, volume, and tempo of our speaking. Interestingly, our body language accounts for 55 percent of the message (as do symbols). Our tone of voice represents 38 percent of the communication, while the words or content account for a mere 7 percent of the message we send! Notice that we tend to put most of our attention on the smallest portion of the communication package—the words!

SOME BASIC GROUND RULES

Effective communication will be the result of a combination of awareness, respect, conscious choice, and openness. These themes are important to carry with you into your conversations.

Awareness is all about being attentive and alert, paying full attention to each other. Listen to what the other is saying, and also 'listen' with your eyes and your intuition. Be present and listen without judgment or criticism.

Respect is a matter of noticing that the one you are speaking with is unique, with their own universe of understanding, opinions, beliefs, thoughts, and feelings. They are not you and do not experience the world the way you do. Respecting that person for their uniqueness goes along way towards creating a healthy environment for deeper communication.

Consciously choosing to communicate is powerful. We often find ourselves in the middle of a conversation wondering how we got there. Making a conscious choice to communicate with another person sets a strong intention, and enables real conversations to take place.

Openness is a practice of bringing a fresh and curious mind to the exchange, being willing to *see* the person and what they share as new and interesting. The attitude of openness is felt, and creates space for people to be themselves. Its opposite, the state of being closed, shuts down the free flow of conversation and has people less willing to speak their truth.

COMMUNICATION TOOLS

Here are some basic tools to help great communication to take place. Remember that these tools will work best when you also create an environment that includes the values mentioned above.

To demonstrate that you understand the feelings embedded in the speaker's message you can use a tool called *empathy*, reflecting back your perception of their feelings. An example would be:

"I notice in your eyes and by the tone in your voice the sadness and grief you feel about your recent loss."

Clarifying what you have heard is a great tool to let the speaker know you have heard them, and is also a good way to gain deeper understanding. To clarify a statement you would ask open-ended questions. *Paraphrasing* is similar and it is also used to show the speaker you have understood their message. Paraphrasing is simply restating the message using your own words. Here are two examples—first a clarifying question followed by a paraphrase:

"How do you feel when you are sitting in a hospital room beside your father?"

"What I heard you say was you feel uncomfortable and confused."

Sometimes when you are talking with people, they may communicate a lot of information all at once in disorderly fashion. To let them know you are with them in the conversation and to help them get clear on exactly what they are saying, you can use a tool to help them *summarize* what they have said. You help them to communicate the gem or core of the more drawn-out message. To help someone achieve this type of clarity is extremely helpful. Simply have them recap the major point(s) they were making; if they can't, you could recap it for them. Here is a model of how it could sound:

"Mary, you just shared a lot of information with me. Could you recap it for me so I can understand the core of what you are saying?"

The "*I*" *Message* is one of the key rules of healthy, full, and open communication. Practice speaking from your own perspective, or using "I". Many times in social and business conversation you will here people talking about others. They will use words like you, them, or those people. Speaking about others by using these types of "you" words is very common. Unfortunately, that perspective is not very helpful when it comes to communication that works, as it can seem confrontational to the listener.

Here are some examples of **common social language;**

"You know, when you have to face your Dad's death, you get quite upset and it makes you confused and scared. Sometimes you don't know what you should do."

In this example, you may guess correctly that they are speaking about themselves, but it can be and is confusing. There is a much clearer way to speak about yourself.

"I" messages can sound like this;

"When I am faced with my father's death I feel upset, scared and confused. I don't know what to do."

The difference can be heard and felt immediately. There is no mistaking what or whom the person is talking about. When you are with people who tend to talk in the safe and social way it is best to find a way to guide them to speak more clearly about themselves as opposed to the safety of "you". This will engage the person speaking, and have them claim their personal power through the way they speak.

Here is a hint or two:

In response to the common social language example above you could respond by saying something like this:

"Yes I know it must be difficult for you to face your Dad's death. Tell me a bit more about how it is for you."

In this way you are acknowledging what they said by re-phrasing their comments in your own words. Then gently lead them back to themselves by instructing them to tell you more about how it is for them. It will take some time. Your continued support, and your gentle guidance will help them say what is real for them.

Another suggestion is to model how you would like them to explain themselves by speaking that way yourself. Always present your own thoughts, feelings, and emotions from the perspective of you using 'I' statements.

GETTING INTO THE CONVERSATION

There are multiple pieces to the messages people send each other and this is oftentimes why we have misunderstandings. There is the verbal component of the message which accounts for a surprisingly small 7 percent of the communication, the non-verbal (body language) portion which is 38 percent, and the largest portion 55 percent is the para-verbal component, all the emotional and energetic content of what we are communicating.

It is important to bear these in mind when talking with each other, especially in times of stress and emotion. You will need to listen with all your faculties, hearing what others are saying, watching for their body language while empathically feeling their emotions.

TALKING ABOUT IT

Another hint: the words *listen* and *silent* have the same letters. When listening to someone it is good to be silent and not interrupt! There are two parts to a conversation: speaking and listening. These two actions are interdependent and are equally important. Especially during times of emotion, it is necessary to observe the basic principle of not interrupting the speaker. Give them their airtime; when they are finished, just switch roles, so that you talk and they listen.

Most people get so involved in conversations that they stop listening and interrupt to get their two cents worth in. It is essential to have them wait for you to finish before they talk again. Correcting an interruption could sound like this;

"I know you are excited to get your point across to me and I would like to finish my thought before you carry on, so please hold your thought 'til I'm done. Thanks."

It is important to establish this listening and speaking flow, as it will greatly improve mutual understanding. Patience, trust, and respect will rise—along with the feeling of caring—the more you can practice the non-interruption principle.

WATCHING IT

Now that you have the conversation going and there is a flow to it, you can start to notice the various facets of communication that are always going on. Most of us simply have not been trained in this area, so we fail to notice all the unspoken messages flying around in the form of body language, emotional energy, and voice tones.

When we are in difficult and emotional conversations our bodies tend to give signals to others about what is really going on for us. These body communications can be very helpful when we pay attention to them and use them as additional information. Watch for such things as eye contact, facial expressions, body position, fidgeting, and breath. All these hints will help create a much more complete message than just paying attention to the words.

Here is an example:

The person you are talking with has just said something like:

"Well, I'm OK, just holding it together as best as I can."

And as they are speaking you notice that they are holding their breath and fighting back the tears, fidgeting, biting nails, or not making eye contact.

This is helpful information and you could respond by saying something like this:

"Bill, I get you are doing your best to keep it together. I can't help but notice, though, that you are holding your breath and your eyes are watering. Is there something you need to say?"

Another example:

Bill responds to your inquiry above by crossing his arms, pulling back in his chair and stiffening his lips while saying,

"No, not really."

Bill's words and body language seem to be out of sync, and you could continue one of two ways. (Remember, communication is an art form and requires sensitivity and creativity. It is not a science, so there is no one right formula.) It appears that he is withholding something, and it is fair to assume he could be. Depending on the setting you are in, who else is around, and how well you know him, you might choose to let it go for now and continue with a more comfortable conversation. You could as easily choose to continue to press forward a little and see what happens.

"Bill, I know this conversation is difficult, and that it must be hard for you to keep it all together. It is fine with me if you let go a little bit here, and you might feel better if you do."

Bill will respond one of two ways. He will let go a little, in which case you can just receive him without making a big deal about it, while simply acknowledging what he presents to you. The other option is that Bill will continue to hold it together, in which case you would pull back a bit and allow the conversation to stay in his safe and comfortable zone.

All that is required to be a great communication artist is thoughtfulness and practice!

FEELING IT

Now that you have the conversation happening, and you are watching body language and non-verbal messages more closely, we can put our attention on the voice tone and emotional energy component (the para-verbal portion) and dive a little deeper into a more full and satisfying conversation.

When surrounding death and dying, there is a lot going on! Generally, people are trying to be polite and not add to the pain or emotion of the moment—or conversely, they have lost it and are an emotional wreck. Many of us don't really know what to say. The taboo around speaking openly and lovingly is because we simply haven't been taught.

Here are a few basics pointers when dealing with emotions expressed or unexpressed:

There is nothing wrong with emotions. As a matter of fact, there is everything right with them! Holding back emotions can result in physical and mental illness over time, while excessive expression can be a big avoidance and a passive/aggressive way to get attention and love. Finding the balance without forcing or resisting is the artful sweet spot we are looking for.

In the world of emotions, do not expect common sense, because you won't find it! The best approach I have found is to simply receive the emotions as they are expressed. Once the emotional expression is complete and you have received it, the energy will settle down and you can get back to the conversation at hand. Remember, emotions and rational thoughts oftentimes don't mix.

Now that you have some solid basics to work with, let's continue to add a few more tools to your toolbox.

GETTING OTHERS TO TALK

Show them how by your own choice of words and phrases. It is very likely that the people you are talking with have no idea how to talk about death. Many may not want to discuss it at all because it can feel so uncomfortable. Others simply don't know what to say and don't want to make things worse by saying what they fear will be the wrong thing.

You can model sentences for them and guide them to speak more openly about what is going on by simply doing it yourself. Here are several examples of sentences you could try. Remember this is my way of speaking, so find your own words and phrases using these as a template of sorts. Here is a tip: the most important ingredient is gentle, loving compassion, and sincere care for the person with whom you are talking. When people feel your care and support, they will be much more likely to open up to a different conversation about death.

"I know talking about your husband's imminent death is scary and awkward. I used to be frightened about it too!"

"I know this may feel uncomfortable for you, but let's have a talk about how you are doing with you father's health and likely death."

"I know our family wants to avoid talking about Harry's terminal illness, but I think it would be good to try."

You could also use sentences like this to demonstrate how they could express themselves:

"When I first heard the news that Sally had only three months to live I was scared, shocked, sad, and all mixed up. I really was confused and upset."

"When I was sitting by Mom's bedside yesterday, comforting her and holding her hand, I got all choked up and sad thinking she may not be around much longer."

"I couldn't believe I was so angry at Dad when I heard he was dying of cancer. I was really pissed off at him."

Speaking to others this way gives them permission to self-reflect and say what they are really feeling and thinking. Your example can help them express what they otherwise may have stuffed down. Again, these three sentences are my way of speaking. Use them as a type of formula and create your own sentences.

By using these examples, you are providing a great role model. The next step is to gently draw them out into the conversation and get them talking.

Here are some more examples:

"How are you doing with the news of Dad's death?"

"What happens for you when you sit beside Mom holding her hand knowing that she can't talk with you?"

"How are you dealing with all the medical staff pushing and prodding every fifteen minutes?"

You will notice that these three examples do not allow for a *yes* or a *no* answer. They are called *open questions* and are designed to encourage people to open up to what is going on inside them. If you approach someone who is having challenges speaking out by asking a question they can answer with a *yes* or a *no,* they will take the opportunity to give you the shortest possible answer—a *yes* or a *no.*

Being the communication guide in a conversation, it is important for you to express your understanding to the speaker. Understanding is easier to express than you may think, and can be a simple as "Oh I get it," or "Yes, tell me some more." Often it can be as non-invasive as a simple nod!

Many people often don't understand what they are feeling or thinking, so when they speak they often feel that they aren't making sense. When you acknowledge them and what they are saying, two things happen. Firstly, they feel relieved. They spoke out and someone understood them, and that helps them let go of what they otherwise could have carried around unsaid for years! Secondly, with their first thought understood, it gives them the confidence to share even more. Feeling not judged, criticized, or corrected, they are much more willing to continue the conversation. This unconditional listening is truly a powerful and loving gift you can offer loved ones.

Working with people in the realm of communication is, as I have said, an art form. How to draw out the whole truth as they understand it and support them in their most full and complete self-expression is the ultimate communication art! Drawing out these more difficult emotions takes practice and skill. It may require the aid of a hospice volunteer, or in some cases, a therapist. My point here is that there are often deeper emotions and thoughts lurking below the surface that may require additional support. Asking for professional help in situations like this is a sign of both wisdom and courage, not a sign of failure or weakness.

TALKING WITH THE FAMILY

You will find yourself in a group of family and friends around the time of death, and when the family usually gets together. You will notice some of your family and friends are outspoken, while others seldom talk. During times such as death it is important to help people speak up and share what is going on for them. In our culture, speaking out is often that last thing we would choose to do given the taboo around speaking openly about death. For the person who is more naturally quiet, an invitation to share is often needed.

If you are in a group and notice the conversation being dominated by a couple of people, you could take a chance and try to include the quiet ones by saying something like this:

"Boy, it has been a great chat. Would anyone who hasn't had a chance to share like to say something?"

You have just gently invited the more soft-spoken individuals to chip in. By creating this opportunity, you are doing your best to include everyone and give people time to say what is in their heart and on their mind. Even if they remain silent, which is their choice, you have acknowledged them as a member of the group. Important stuff!

TAKING CARE OF YOURSELF

I was a passenger on an airplane the other week, and for the first time in a while, I paid attention to the pre-flight safety demonstration. I noticed the part when the oxygen masks dropped down; the instruction was to put your own mask on first, then the mask for your children. What a great life lesson!

It highlighted for me the need to take good care of one's self, especially in times of emotional, physical, and spiritual stress, such as dealing with the loss of a loved one. So I created this section to remind you of some of the self-care steps you can take. By taking great care of yourself, you will be much more able to take care of loved ones!

PHYSICAL CARE

Make sure you get some physical exercise, and some outdoor time. There is a lot going on around you, with many details to handle, lots of people to be with, and many emotional conversations to have. It can be draining physically. Be sure to drink plenty of water, get rest, and take catnaps when you can. Get plenty of sleep, and eat well—even if your appetite is low. Remember to honor your own physical limitations ,and when you need to take a rest or a break say so, especially to yourself.

EMOTIONAL CARE

Find some support for yourself, a friend, or family member who can be there for you. Local hospice societies provide volunteers who are well-trained in grief and loss, so take advantage of that service if it is available. Remember, you too have the right to your own unique expression of grief and the fullness of your own emotions. Emotional expression is a way to maintain your emotional health. Suppressing your emotions, and holding them back—though it may seem to make the goings easier—will ultimately have you feeling ill at ease with yourself, and doesn't serve you in the long run.

MENTAL CARE

There will be so much going through the minds of family and friends; some of those things will be understandable, and some will be confusing and unclear. These shared thoughts may trigger some of your own confusion. It is fine to have your own ideas as you do your best to understand it all and to put it into a paradigm that makes sense. Using a journal could help you organize and collect it all. Remember, it is okay to have your own personal thoughts about the loss.

SPIRITUAL CARE

Death often brings up the issue of spirituality. *Who am I? Who was my loved one? What is life? What is the point of it all?* These questions are deeply spiritual and well worth asking. It is perfectly fine if you are inspired to use ceremony and ritual to help you through your own grief journey. These rituals help and also bring people close to you for added support. Remember—ritual and ceremony is a personal choice that you have the right to make.

"Those who have learned to love life find it easier to embrace death. Like water evaporating from a saucer, they melt into its arms, peacefully and without resistance. Both in living and in dying, they inspire countless others"—Nithya Shanti

CHAPTER SEVEN

Musings from the Compassionate Couch
Different Ways to Talk About Death

The call of death is a call of love. Death can be sweet if we answer it in the affirmative, if we accept it as one of the great eternal forms of life and transformation.—Hermann Hesse

Here is a collection of my articles on the many facets of death, all from the perspective of embracing death and being inspired to live an even richer life.

KEEPING THEIR SPIRIT ALIVE

DEATH-INSPIRED GOALS

I remember clearly the moment I was lowering my younger sister's body into her gravesite. I made a solemn oath that her death would not be in vain. I committed to discover the truth about life and death. I intended to make sense out of Jody's passing. I set a goal!

Looking back at this intention, I noticed that this was a way I began to make sense of Jody's unexpected and sudden death. In a way, it gave meaning to her death, and it helped me along my journey to acceptance of her passing. In a very direct way it breathed a new sense of life into me.

Here are a few of the commitments I made as a result of my own experience of the unexpected loss of a loved one:

- I intended to stay closer with my entire family.
- Tell my children more often how much I love them and how proud I am of them.
- Write books that would help people.
- Change my career.

Setting a personal goal as a result of the loss of a loved one is a real way to honor their death by creating new life. My goal to make sense out of life and death ultimately resulted in this book! The death of my sister equals birth of this book.

In the case of death, a new life or a new sense of life must emerge somewhere in the family unit.

Once the busy times surrounding the death have settled and you have a bit of breathing room and personal time, I encourage you to create for yourself some goals which are inspired by your loss. These goals can reflect a realization you have gained, an insight, or learning resulting from the death.

Take a look at any regrets that arise for you when you think about your loved one. Here are some common regrets people close to death often speak about. This list is part of a wonderful book by Bonnie Ware.

- I wish I'd had the courage to live my life, not the life others expected of me.
- I wish I didn't work so hard.
- I wish I'd had the courage to express myself more fully.
- I wish I had stayed in touch with my friends and family.
- I wish that I had expressed to others the happiness I felt.

There are many other regrets that folks nearing death often experience, and I am sure if you recall conversations with the loved one you can add to this basic list.

Here is what you can do with these gems of wisdom. For example: Your loved one expressed that they wished they had stayed in touch with friends and family. If this regret moved you and you feel inspired to live your life differently you could set a goal such as:

- I will call each of my family members at least once each month.

Whatever regrets you feel might end up coming out of your mouth as you prepare for your own death would be good goals to set right now. Once you have created these goals, make sure to let your friends and family know so they can support you in accomplishing them. Perhaps your actions will inspire them to join you in remembering all of your loved ones in this unique way.

Setting great life goals that are inspired by the loss of a loved one is a genuine way to honor their life wisdom and keep their spirit alive in you.

WHY ARE WE AFRAID OF DEATH?

WE LEFT THE FARM!

I was wondering the other day why our culture is so in denial about death; why are we so frightened to even talk about it? I believe that the behavior of a person always makes sense if you can get under their skin and learn of the history they were raised in. So I set out to understand why North Americans have this tendency to avoid death at all costs.

As I pondered this issue I remembered my childhood, growing up in the fifties. I recalled summers on my uncle's farm in the Ottawa Valley, fitting right in with family life. What this meant to me was great meals, boating, and tons of farm duties while enjoying life!

In hindsight, though, I realize what was happening on a more subtle level. I was living much more in the natural flow of life, the cycles of life as so beautifully demonstrated in the show Lion King: planting of the seeds, care of the crops, harvesting, then Thanksgiving. The birth of piglets the feeding and tending them was followed by the slaughter, and the resulting food. On the farm, nature was very much a part of everyday life, as were we. Birth, life, and death were not separate.

Life and death were common. They were taken as normal and natural occurrences. Sometimes an animal would die, and in its own way, the family would say good-bye and set the animal to rest. At other times the animal was slaughtered for food or for sale. No matter what the case, the animal was always treated with love and respect, and the death was just another part of life.

Looking back at those summers, I saw the cycles regularly; birth and death were bookends of the same life, and they were nothing to be afraid of or to deny. We demonstrated our acceptance of life's cycles by such simple practices as celebrating the end of each day, and the end of a season by honoring the solstice.

These early experiences laid a solid foundation and understanding of death, and yet my family's approach to loss, along with friends and society's, buried this groundwork under a flood of confusion, fear, and denial. When dealing with my own family's loss, my therapist was able to tap into this, helping me through the journey of grief.

Noticing my now relaxed and calm approach compared to the more common approach of fear and denial, I hopped on my trusty laptop and looked into the demographics of Canada and how they have changed over the years. I compared the rural population with those of us living in the cities. I discovered a trend that is also common in other countries like India and China: rural dwellers move to the larger cities to find work and money for their families. The significance was not the trend from rural to urban living; more significantly, it was the magnitude of the migration. Here is what I discovered:

- In 1800, 97 percent of us lived in the country.
- By 1851, 87 percent of Canada's population lived rurally—a change of 10 percent over fifty years.
- One hundred years later, in 1951, those of us living in cities and rurally was about balanced—fifty-fifty.
- Over the course of 200 years, there was a decline of 47 percent in rural population.
- Over the next sixty-year period, from 1951 to 2011, the rural population dropped to only 17 percent—a stunning reversal in lifestyle.

This trend is demonstrated by a story I remember back in the early 2000s. I was hosting some young city kids at my home on the semi rural Sunshine

Coast of BC. It was late summer and we were busy preparing a great feast. We needed more lettuce for the salad. I asked one of the city kids if he would get some lettuce for us. He asked for the car keys. When I asked him why, he said, "To go to the store and get some lettuce." I took him to the deck overlooking the garden and pointed to the lettuce patch that he had tended earlier in the day. The assumption on his part was that food simply comes from the store.

These phenomena, a massively digital world, this move to urban living and all that cities have to offer has put a huge percentage of our population out of touch with the natural cycle of life and death—so much so that both births and deaths now occur primarily in hospitals or care facilities. Our culture has made pathology out of two of nature's most natural events.

Though most Canadians (70 percent), want to die at home, most deaths occur out of the home environment, usually behind closed doors in a hospital or care facility. Death has become an enemy, something to fight to the last gasp, something to avoid because we are afraid to experience it directly or indirectly. We are simply out of touch with the natural flow of life. In order to get back to basics with the beautiful cycles of birth and death, here are a few practices you can try.

- Plant a family garden of some sort.
- Go for walks in nature—a park, by a river, lake or ocean if possible.
- Make a practice of ending each day consciously.
- Welcome the beginning of each day with a simple personal ritual.
- Take a farm tour.
- Shop at a farmer's market and shake hands with the growers.
- Celebrate the change of our seasons with a gathering or party.
- In a more conscious way, acknowledge the beginning and ending of each month.

These simple practices will help you get back in touch in a mindful way with all the unique births and deaths life has to offer. A regular habit of acknowledging beginnings and endings will help you stay present to the very natural flow of life from start to finish.

WHEW, THAT WAS INTENSE!
PREPARE FOR THE POST SUPPORT LULL

Most often when death occurs there is a fair bit of support; medical and professional staff from the health care system, expert staff from the funeral home, and perhaps hospice or therapy if needed. There is usually strong support from friends, family members, and co-workers too. Everyone is focused on the tasks at hand and, generally speaking, very supportive.

As time passes, and the funeral ceremony is complete, the level of support starts to naturally dwindle. Obviously the help from the health care system winds down, and professional support from the funeral home or crematorium ends. The support from friends and family slowly diminishes as everyone gets back to their own lives.

In a matter of days, more often weeks, the beehive of activity subsides, and everything and everyone—including you—is expected to get back to normal. All of a sudden, you may feel like you are on your own, and in many cases you can be. Friends at work may not know what to say to you, and may hang back because they don't want to upset you. Neighbors may get back to life as it was before the death. Many people may be done with their own grief process, though you may not be. You could feel alone in your post-funeral slump.

Although this is not intentional, it is often quite a predictable path. Knowing this and not taking it personally, you can expect this lull in contact, support, and attention. In order to prepare for this change, make plans for you and your family to spend quality time together. Help your children plan sleepovers and outings with friends. Create enjoyable events and gatherings for yourself too! These are not to distract you from your natural grief process; it is more to bring a better balance back in to your life.

If you are living alone, it can be a real shock to go from close quarters and lots of contact with others to being on your own. It can be easy to slip into a lonely life and a form of depression. Be sure to set up get-togethers with friends, co-workers, and family. You could join a social group or exercise club and continue with spiritual activities.

Again, this strategy is not to avoid healthy alone time when you can grieve on your own; rather, it is to make sure you have good balance in your life. Too much contact can be overwhelming, and too much alone time can be avoidance. If you have a tendency to be a bit of a lone wolf, it might be a good idea to ask your close friends to help you create a well-balanced social calendar for a month or two after the death, and to give you a gentle nudge if you seem to be withdrawing.

Either way, living in a family setting or alone, it is important to expect the post-funeral slump in attention and support and also in your mental state. This awareness and some good planning will help you regain important balance in your changed life.

WHAT IS WRONG WITH ME?
AM I DEPRESSED?

After giving birth, some mothers fall into a period of postpartum depression resulting from a change of body chemistry, and in a way, the end (death) of the pregnancy. Similarly, with death of a loved, one there can be a bout of depression following the loss. It is important to be aware of this potential healthcare issue.

Here are some signs to keep a lookout for as you are moving along your own journey of grief. It is supportive to watch out for these same signals in your family and close friends who have suffered a loss. This by no means is a comprehensive list, but they are the more common signs.

If you have a number of these signs and they occur regularly, it would be a good idea to make a visit to your family doctor or therapist and get some professional advice and an informed opinion.

1. **Sleep**
You are sleeping more than normal and have trouble getting out of bed, or perhaps you are not sleeping much at all and are getting fatigued.

2. **Aches, pains, and illness**
Your body is more achy and painful than usual, and you may have more colds or illnesses than you normally do.

3. **Excessive use of drugs or alcohol**
In order to get some relief from your feelings, or to hide your deeper emotions, you may resort to the excessive use of alcohol. This is very common with people suffering from depression. You may choose illicit or prescription drugs to help numb the emotions that so often accompany grief.

4. **Weight change**
Your weight may drop noticeably as your appetite vanishes, or you may use food to suppress your feelings and emotions and gain some.

5. **Work**
Are regularly absent from work or late? You might also notice you are not as productive as you were before the loss or have trouble concentrating. The opposite is also possible: over-working and over-achieving as a way to keep you busy and distracted, which indicates avoidance.

6. **General lack of motivation**
You just are not motivated to do anything, even hobbies that you once loved. It might even show up in a lack of sex drive.

7. **Anxiety**
Levels of anxiety can appear that you haven't experienced before. This may not have a basis to it and may even turn into types of panic attacks.

8. **Emotions**
You could experience a low-grade sense of irritability and edginess that from time to time that shows up as anger. Anger is often an outward sign of fear or hurt.

9. **Thoughts of death or suicide**
You could experience thoughts of taking your own life and become pre-occupied with musings of death—both yours, and others.

I was once asked what is the opposite of depression. I had to ponder it at length and avoid my initial reaction to blurt out the word joy. As I looked at the question more fully it came to me that the opposite of depression is *expression*.

Some of us who are depressed oftentimes feel flat, lifeless, and dead in a way. When we look more deeply, we notice a cauldron of emotions lying just underneath the surface of our flatness. Sometimes dropping into the sea of emotions and expressing them can be a healing and also freeing event—an event that may also lift the depression.

MY BODY MAY BE DEAD BUT...
GETTING THE DIGITAL ME IN ORDER.

My friend Laura Markley sent me a link to a very interesting conference: Digital Death Day, being held in Amsterdam. Here is what the conference is all about:

(This quote was taken from the marketing flyer put out by the organizing team.)

> *DEATH IS A PART OF LIFE AND LIFE HAS (TO AN EXTENT) BECOME DIGITAL.*
>
> *Our increasing digitality means that we will increasingly be forced to come FACE to SCREEN with the various dimensions and complexities of Digital Death.*

There was also an article in recent NUVO magazine entitled "Data After Death" that was pondering the same issue: what happens to all our posts, blogs, and digital identity? What sorts of considerations are there when it comes to taking care of your digital life after your physical death?

Do the digital remains get turned over to the estate? What about my business digital data? Of all my digital remains, which ones are private and which ones are public? Are emails different than a blog post? What about Facebook, LinkedIn, and Twitter? Is my digital persona bound by the same laws as my physical body?

There are many questions to be answered about such things as how to handle important documents stored on your computer, passwords for online banking, and email access. What about online dollars in PayPal accounts and other shopping services? How about online subscriptions?

I don't have the answers. In fact I have lots of questions. What I am doing, though, is making sure that key information such as passwords, accounts, websites, and email addresses are recorded and kept in a safe place such as a safety deposit box.

Getting the digital me in order!

AS LIFE WINDS DOWN
OUT AND ABOUT NO MORE

It is indeed a journey from the moment you learn that you are dying until the instant you pass on. Sometimes it is as the Beatles once sang, a long and winding road, at other times it is short and bumpy, and at other times it is in between and smooth. There is no one way that a prognosis moves from being identified to it being fulfilled. Each person's path is totally unique.

There are, however, some common stages that we all move through, much like a travel itinerary. The exact details may differ, yet the day-to-day road map is similar. In palliative care, the doctors and nursing staff have identified the following stages that a person often passes through. I thought it worthwhile that you have this information too. Understanding the flow from identifying a terminal illness to death can literally be life-saving for those of us saying good-bye.

The six key stages are listed. Firstly, notice the impact each has on the person, and secondly on family and friends. It is common that everyone reacts differently to similar news and it is important to recognize these different reactions if we are to take good care of each other.

1. **In the Beginning: The Diagnosis**
   Patient
   When you first hear the news of a terminal illness there can be many reactions. Common amongst patients are denial, disbelief, a feeling of uncertainty, confusion, anger, and fear.
   Family and Friends
   People will react differently depending from whom they hear the news. If it is from the ill family member they may not hear the whole story, so there may be denial, confusion, and lots of questions. There may be some conflict as each friend or family member may have different beliefs and ideas, and therefore interpret the facts from their own personal perspective.

2. **It is for Real**
   Patient
   At this stage there may be fatigue as normal activities become tougher to complete. There may be some grief surrounding the loss of some faculties like mobility or perhaps sight. The person may begin to doubt the treatments. Thoughts about death may occur and the individual may begin to feel isolated and lonely.
   Family and Friends
   Family and friends may start to look and sound like cheerleaders as they notice the changes and want to inspire and give hope to their loved one. They might start looking for alternative treatments and they could begin to look towards imminent death. They may also get back to their own life and create

some distance between themselves and their loved one. This could be the result of avoidance or fear.

3. **Shifting to Pain Management**
   Patient

At this point the one dying will likely be losing some more mobility and control of their body. They could be more fatigued, weak, and less active mentally and physically. Your loved one may be more confused and looking towards prayer, hope for a spiritual healing, and sometimes even death just to get some comfort. They may have feelings of shame and guilt for 'letting' their loved ones down.

   Family and Friends

After living with uncertainty for sometime now, family and friends may look for other solutions, especially as care demands increase. Caregivers often look for ways to find some stability and control in their own lives and their resentment can reach a high level as even more care may be necessary.

4. **Care Demands Increase**
   Patient

Your loved one now is mostly bedridden and will need help with personal care. Their appetite and thirst will be lessening. When coupled with increased medications due to more complex health needs you may find them drowsy. The one dying will likely be trying to make meaning of it all and be preparing for death. Their world is shrinking and their energy is diminishing. Care must be taken to spread out visits and activity.

5. *Family and Friends*

At this point you may be wondering how much longer it will go on. *Can we continue to do this?* You may get so focused on caregiving that you forget to take good care of yourself. There may be even more demands of you as visitors come by more often to say their final good-byes.

Final Steps
   Patient

The body and mind will be changing rapidly and these can be profound. They may not eat or drink and may slip into a coma. Your loved one could be restless, become even more confused, and they may not have much mental clarity. Pain cannot always be controlled, which is a harsh reality for all.

6. *Family and Friends*

As death nears, family and friends may be going in many directions; some are ready for death to come, while some are holding on for dear life. Feelings such as anger, guilt, sadness, and hopeless could surface. Others may be relieved, thankful, and peaceful. It will likely be difficult to communicate with your loved one at this point, and simply sitting, holding hands and talking may be the extent of your communications. Hearing, by the way, is the last faculty to go, making speaking to your loved one very important. However, lots of uncertainty will be in the air as family and friends start to let go.

7. **Death**

Patient

Your loved one may go quietly and calmly, or they may be restless and the death could be dramatic. Either way, death comes.

8. *Family and Friends*

Though it has been a journey, and the expected destination has always been death, it may still be a shock when it happens. Panic and fear, relief and peacefulness can all emerge. Some family and friends could withdraw, while others may be expressive. Some folks could leave, and others stay closer by. It is usually a time for family to stay close together.

© 2012 barbara cameron pix

LIFT YOURSELF OUT OF THE FOG...

DO MEN GRIEVE DIFFERENTLY THAN WOMEN?
HELL YES!

It is very obvious that men and women are different physically; less obvious are the differences spiritually and emotionally. David Deida has written extensively about these fundamental differences in two of his books, *Dear Lover* and *Way of the Superior Man*. It is important to recognize that we all have both masculine and feminine energy, so none of us will be all one way or the other. We will each be a unique blend with our own preferences when it comes to grieving.

It is also important to know that there are commonalities amongst grieving men that are different from women. I will explore what it often looks like for men, what men tend to do with grief, and how to support the grieving man.

Know that these different tendencies arise for many reasons: cultural upbringing (the John Wayne syndrome); differences in male and female brains both functionally and anatomically are two of the major contributors. It is important to recognize that each man has his own unique grief journey, and though we can draw some general conclusions, each man will have his own signature.

WHAT TO LOOK FOR IN MEN

Though men may express 'typical' signs of grief such as hopelessness, sadness, crying, or depressed moods, they do so much less than women often because society generally demands a stiff upper lip. More typically you will find men displaying symptoms that are rare in women.

- *Irritability:* Whether he is your partner, friend, co-worker, son, or father the grieving man may have a feeling of underlying irritability. You may sense this in his demeanor or in the way he talks. He may feel 'chippy' or resentful and overreact to small upsets.
- *Anger:* Sometimes a man will direct his anger at what he feels was the cause of the death. Other times he will direct it inwards or simply be angry at everything in general.
- *Withdrawal:* Men will from time to time pull back from social outings. They may also feel numb and distant as they withdraw emotionally as well.
- *Intellectualizing:* Some men may spend a fair bit of time mulling over their life with their deceased loved one. Others may think about death in general.
- *Substance Misuse:* Some men may turn to alcohol or drugs in an attempt to manage their emotions to help them get some 'rest' from the feelings of grief.

These more masculine ways may lead to conflict both internally and in relationships. His female partner may misunderstand his grief and try to get him to grieve more like her, trying to get him to talk it all through. Internally, the man may feel as if he is not grieving the right way.

Though most men grieve for shorter periods than do their female counterparts, there is no exact time frame for male grief. This journey will vary widely from man to man, some being short periods—perhaps months—and other grieving for years, or perhaps a lifetime.

WHAT MEN TEND TO DO

Most men tend to be problem solvers and Mr. Fixit. They want to get the tasks done, so they approach grief in a similar manner. Guys also tend to control their emotions and rely on their own inner strengths. What this means is that men will likely not respond to grief support groups. For example, at a training program for hospice volunteers I recently attended there were twenty participants: seventeen women and three men. The facilitator was female and all the guest presenters were women. A quick tour of hospice web sites shows the same bias. Staff and volunteer teams are predominantly women.

Clearly men handle losses by doing their 'grief work' differently. Action, thinking, and fixing will be the more typical male responses to grief. It is important to recognize that the more female approaches to grief are necessary as well. A man needs to find balance between coping emotionally and coping by restoring life to order.

When men don't find healthy ways to express their grief in a way that works for them, you may notice men feeling unseen or misunderstood in their grief and tending to keep it all a secret. They may appear complete with their grief, but don't be fooled.

HANDY TIPS FOR MEN

- *Give yourself permission to grieve your own way:* Each man will have his own way of expressing his grief than he may have expected. It may surprise others too. As long as there is no harm being done to himself or those around him, allowing his authentic expression of grief will help the healing process.
- *Get together with your good men friends:* It is healing also for men to get together and support each other either informally or in a men's support group. Being with other men who have gone through a similar loss is especially helpful. This could be the source of his strongest support.
- *Pay attention to your actions:* Two areas to pay attention to are the expression of anger and the use of alcohol or drugs. Refrain from using anger as a weapon to hurt others with, and find healthy ways to express it. Notice a man's coping tools, and be aware of excessive use of alcohol or drugs that may be used to mask the uncomfortable emotions common with grief.
- *Ask for help:* Men seeking support can be seen as weak or a failure. Notice harmful or self-damaging behavior and reach out for professional support to help get through the tough times.

HOW TO SUPPORT THE GRIEVING MAN

- *Simply be there and just listen:* Sometimes just sitting with a man, being present and quiet is the best support you can offer. When a man is emotionally full, adding words to his universe may not be helpful. Letting him know you are there for him and willing to help is important. Avoid problem-solving and providing advice.
- *Let him express his loss in his way:* Follow his lead and create space for him to grieve in his way, which is likely much different than yours. When dancing, only one partner can lead. If you want to avoid stepping on your partner's toes let him lead. Grief is a dance, too!
- *Take good care of yourself:* Grief can be intense and fatiguing. Make sure you get good rest and take care of yourself. If you're tired, you're of no help.
- *Be prepared to ask for help if needed:* Generally speaking, most men will get through the grief process without the need for outside support. If help is needed, know when to ask for it.

YOU CAN TRUST YOUR DEATH!
REALLY?

I have noticed over the years all the signs and signals that generally make death our adversary. A recent television advertisement that carries the statement "Make death wait" reminded me of our tendency to see death as a foe, something we need to delay at the minimum, and something to usually fight against vigorously with all manner of 'weapons'.

As I look around at the world and see all that we do to avoid aging: plastic surgery, a shot of Botox, a pinch here and a lift there. We seem to be demonstrating that we think we have some degree of mastery or power over one of life's certain yet mysterious events—death.

Now don't get me wrong—I love life and value it deeply. I am not interested in rushing my death at all. I wholeheartedly agree with good nutrition, good exercise, good spiritual practice, and taking care of ourselves so we can enjoy life and be able to give ourselves fully to family and friends, to our chosen work, and to our hobbies. When illness comes my way, I do take the steps necessary to return to good health as quickly as possible.

However, I have noticed some things about death, especially in our North American culture, as I pursue a new career in the business of death, both has a volunteer hospice visitor and as a cremationist. I can distill all the activity that pops up around death to one simple sentence: *we don't trust death.*

First, notice all that often goes on when someone you know gets the prognosis that she or he has only months or days to live. Most people opt for one or more of the following solutions:

- Aggressive allopathic treatments
- Extensive naturopathic processes
- Wild and crazy off-the-wall healers
- Radical lifestyle changes
- Tremendous drug regimes
- Spiritual gurus and associated mantras

When death comes knocking, our culture, our healthcare, and alternative care services kick into overdrive! All this activity around death is telling me something.

You know that I have faced the loss of loved ones to death: my sister died in 1988, my father in 2004, and my brother faced and is still facing cancer to this day. My aunt faced a two in ten chance of surviving open-heart surgery and is still with us. Close friends have lost loved ones to suicide. Like many of you, I have first-hand experience with this issue. I understand treatment and pain management and know what I am dealing with here. My understanding comes from very personal and direct experience.

Here is what I have come to understand:

All this activity around aging and death is saying to me that we do not trust death. Somehow death is wrong. We mortals must be able to control it, to manage it to suit our own personal needs and agenda. We ought to be able to master death with all of our technology and knowledge.

What happens if death is *right?*

DEATH, AN INSIDE VIEW

FROM THE PERSPECTIVE OF A CREMATIONIST

Back in 2011 I made a personal commitment to get fully involved in the business of death and dying. It was a calling of sorts. I began volunteering as a hospice visitor, and in early January 2012, I took on a part-time job as a cremationist. I have been fortunate to have lots of opportunities to learn much about the goings-on in a funeral home.

I have had the honor to work with families and their deceased loved ones as they prepare to say their final good-byes—cremation is a fundamental part of that. I have been involved in hundreds of cremations and worked with many families, learning tremendous life lessons by dealing with death first-hand. I have gained insights I would not have otherwise seen, and have been humbled by the reality of death.

I have an understanding of dying, death, grief and loss, and bereavement, have taken hospice training in 1993 and in 2011, and have volunteered. However, working with death so intimately in my career as a cremationist has deepened my personal relationship with death in meaningful ways—so much so that I have taken death on as my life coach!

Death is teaching me daily, each time I sit with a person who is dying, or spend time with the family and friends as they work through pre-grief and grief when the loss comes. Each time I cremate a person and return the cremated remains to the family, I learn something more about life. Here are two stories that illustrate this.

A woman's sister had died unexpectedly. The entire family and their close friends were in shock. I had taken her initial call and helped her begin the process of arranging the cremation and viewing. The arrangements were made, and the day of service had arrived. The chapel was full of family and friends. There was a steady flow of people to the casket to say their final good-byes. The deceased's sister was the last one to pay her respects.

As she completed her visit she turned from the casket and approached me, placing her right hand on my forearm. Looking into my eyes she said, "You will take good care of her, won't you?" In that moment two things struck me: how very much she loved her late sister, and how much trust she had in me to take care of her remains. I am a compassionate and loving fellow, and this lesson taught me to embrace even more deeply how important it is to give great care to loved ones—mine and others.

The second story is about an eighty-six-year-old woman who was close to death. I had met her and her fine husband several times and could feel how much they had cared for each other over the sixty-eight years of their happy marriage. The love they shared was palpable.

He had spent the full day with his wife and was exhausted. He had gone home to rest and get some sleep as he had another full day of caring for her the following day. She was confused and a little frightened when she called down the hall and asked for me to sit with her.

I pulled my chair up close to her bed. I held her hand and gently caressed her head. We spent a fair bit of time just sitting. She liked the physical contact and it settled her.

"Can I tell you something?" she asked.

"Of course." I replied.

"You know, I loved my husband a lot, I am so grateful for him being in my life. He is such a great man and a perfect husband for me. But you know, I held a 'wee bit of my love back from him—I don't know why, I just did, and I find myself wishing I hadn't done that."

I took a deep breath and let her share into my mind and heart. All I could say was, "Thank you."

We sat silently together, and in a while she had fallen asleep. I gently slipped my hand from hers and quietly left her room. As I sat at my desk, I thought what a great gift I had just been given. Here was a wonderfully wise elder sharing with me a beautiful gem of wisdom for living life without regrets. I began to look for where in my life I was holding my love back just a little, and when I found those relationships, I loved them even more.

Here are some other lessons death has taught me about life:

Death is very real. It is physical. No one is getting out alive. I am certain about that, mentally, emotionally, spiritually and physically. I know that one day I will absolutely be dead. This may sound depressing, yet to me it is totally inspiring: I am alive *today!* Today I am breathing and am fully able to experience all that is in front of me! What a gift!

Being right is a waste of time. One of the pastimes many of us enjoy is the pursuit of self-rightness (self-righteousness). I have seen it in my life over and over again. Though common, I find it combative and a waste of time. I'd rather be curious and wrong and learn something about life than be stuck in the land of rightness.

Follow your heart. I spend time with people who are in the final days of their life, and I often hear regrets like "I wish I would have done all those things I wanted to." Sometimes it is spoken like, "I wish I had lived my own life, not the one others wanted me to live." Regrets like these are life lessons turned inside out. For those of us living, hear these lessons and adjust your life so it won't be you talking like that on your deathbed.

Love the one you are with. I was with a family a while back and the sadness was overwhelming. "We all love each other. Sad thing is, we forget to remind ourselves by saying it out loud each day. It is too late to remind Dad." Feel this one—*really* feel it—and if you want to avoid this kind of grief, be more demonstrative with your love today.

Money isn't everything. I have had the honor to cremate many people over the past while—some very wealthy, others very poor. Multi-millionaires to homeless folks, people driving BMWs, and folks pushing shopping carts. When I am done my duty as a cremationist, at the end of the process I can't tell the difference; ashes to ashes, dust to dust. There is no obvious difference in the cremated remains. We all look the same in the end, and there is no evidence of money, stature or possessions.

There's nothing wrong with abundance, and there's nothing right with it either; it just *is*. When it is life-consuming, as in the North American Dream, perhaps it is time to put our attention on what is important: each other.

Death can be very informative when you look at it through new lenses!

Some Buddhist meditations take place in a cemetery, where one is brought closer to the reality of impermanence and the motivation to stay mindful, practice kindness, and wake up!—Joan Borysenko, PhD

... AND INTO THE LIGHT

CHAPTER EIGHT

The Business of Death

Let's Look at the Money

"Remembering that I'll be dead soon is the most important tool I've ever encountered to help me make the big choices in life. Because almost everything—all external expectations, all pride, all fear of embarrassment or failure—these things just fall away in the face of death, leaving only what is truly important. Remembering that you are going to die is the best way I know to avoid the trap of thinking you have something to lose. You are already naked. There is no reason not to follow your heart."—Steve Jobs

---

It is tough to get a good handle on the costs of dying these days. This is in part because of the taboo nature of the topic along with the challenge of finding out the real numbers. There are studies upon studies and articles after articles all over the place. The difficulty is the darn silos in the health care system and the challenge of collecting all the necessary data from the many cost centers within a complex system.

Trying to compare the relative costs of different treatment decisions is in itself a doctoral thesis! Add to these calculations the task of figuring out your health care insurance, additional life, and long-term care provisions and what they all cover and do not cover, and you have the makings of a financial nightmare.

Added to these hard-to-track down healthcare (and alternatives) are the costs of funeral or cremation services; these can also get out of control. While a little easier to track down, when combined with facility and healthcare costs, they can create a demanding financial task.

Imagine a highly emotional time, such as caring for a terminally-ill family member, and add the daunting and often scary burden of money issues. The family has to contend with all of it—logistics and arrangements, money, and emotions. The overload can cause very real decision-making difficulties.

Your rational mind and the emotional mind do not operate very well together. These two facets of the brain are hooked up in such a way that you are generally able to use only one or the other, not both at the same time.

Generally, the emotions of the moment win out and finances are left on the back burner to be handled later. This can be a recipe for poor planning and potential financial shocks for the family to bear on top of the emotional journey already being dealt with.

This part of the book is a basic run-through of the sort of costs that can be incurred. My point in this section is to bring your full attention to the finances of death well in advance so you can prepare a plan for your loved one and yourself that will include compassion, care, and finances that account for the real needs of the family.

I recently read an article from the Global National 2008 containing three short quotations that sum this up:

"People aren't as comfortable with the thought that with life, comes death," said funeral home worker Patrick McGarry. "The death rate is still 100 percent … I think society today is still a death-denying society."

"While some deny it," says McGarry, "others are making it a big business, and with death rates still at 100 percent, the lack of pre-planning and unexpected costs can make it anything but a rest in peace."

Towards the end of the article:

"Because it's such an emotional time we encourage people to bring somebody with them to help with those decisions or help them maybe be a little more objective about those decisions," said Joseph Richer of the Ontario Board of Funeral services. "Or pre-plan your own funeral."

So, to the best of my ability, I have compiled some general financial information that you can use as a guide—areas to consider when you are planning the care program for your loved one. These numbers are ballpark figures that change from health region to health region, from hospital to hospice, and from funeral home to crematorium.

The following are some of the items and services that could be needed in your loved one's care. This list is extensive but by no means complete. I created it so you can understand and grasp all the potential areas you may need to plan for and consider. Yes, it is a lot to hold, and it is important to understand!

END-OF-LIFE CARE CONSIDERATIONS

As I look toward the end of my own life, I am hopeful it will be a graceful and uncomplicated passing—and it may well be, as is the case with many deaths in Canada. That being said, I think it is important to be aware of what could happen, and have a contingency plan for those possibilities just in case. A well-organized plan will save the day and avoid unnecessary confusion and uncertainty. Here are some things I have considered and incorporated into my plans:

I may get a big surprise and things could go differently than I envision. I may be in pain, I may feel sick, I may be dealing with illness terminal or

otherwise. I may lose some of my abilities, my care could get very complicated, and I may become a burden on my family.

I might need to purchase drugs for pain management, to settle my mind if I
become agitated, to help my system if I become congested, and to fight infec-
tion. These drugs could be both allopathic and naturopathic. My preference is
naturopathic, and many of these costs are outside of my health insurance. So
these also need to be considered in my over-all planning.

Depending on how I age, I may require the support of equipment such as
a walker, an oxygen tank, a sheepskin for my sore hips, perhaps a special bed,
potentially a wheel chair or power cart, toilet seat lifts, professionally installed
bath/shower supports, and equipment like a medication pump, or appoint-
ments with a physio or massage therapist. I don't know how it is going to go,
and yet I do need to consider them all as potential possibilities in order for my
family and I to be prepared for what could come our way.

I am no different than most Canadians. I want to die at home in the
comfort of my familiar surroundings, with my friends and family close at hand.
This is my preference and hope, and yet I still need to consider the potential
need for facility care. What type of facility care could I need? Well, there is
long-term care such as a senior's home, hospital care that could be palliative
care, or care in a hospice facility. I need to look at which costs are covered by
my insurance plan(s) and which are not. Can I purchase insurance that would
cover my facility needs, and can I afford it? Could my home be renovated
temporarily, and could those costs be recovered from an insurance plan?

When I looked around at these alternatives, I had a tough time getting
a handle on the costs. What expenses are covered by the health system or
insurance? And which items are not? It was a bit of a challenge, to say the least.
Here are some of the figures I was able to pull together:

Palliative care units include some drugs and physicians' salaries and other
costs, amounting to approximately $425 a day. These, for the most part, are
covered by health insurance. The price of medications, however, are a wild
card in the mix and depend on your health and group insurance and any
additional coverage you may have. Significant cash outlays may be required.

By contrast, though covered by the system, per-diem costs at a *tertiary care
institution* such as a hospital's intensive care unit are roughly $2,900.00 a day.
This estimate includes some drugs and physicians' salaries and staff wages.

At a *hospice unit,* the per-diem amount (excluding drugs, supplies and physicians' care) per patient is roughly $230 per day.

At home it is estimated that an average per diem cost per patient comes
in at $125, although that does not include drugs, equipment, or physicians'
visits. I wonder why our system doesn't encourage this kinder and much more
affordable approach?

My loved one could require some *services* provided by doctors, nurses,
nursing assistants, emergency medical staff plus transportation, personal

support workers, and/or therapists. These costs may not be covered by your insurance plans. For example;

Massage treatments vary in price around the country and you can count on $75.00 for a one-hour session. Physiotherapy sessions cost roughly $50.00.

When I review all these variables and costs for my family and me, I realize how important it is to have solid plans in place that are based on accurate cost estimates and careful consideration. While doing research for this book, I discovered that British Columbia, Canada has a *palliative care benefit program* that can be accessed by the family when there is a prognosis of life ending within six months. This program affords the individual amongst other benefits, free medication, some equipment and nursing visits. This type of investigating can go a long way to making a challenging time easier.

Moving on, let's look at all the potential options and costs that you will need to consider once death has occurred. These are easier to pin down and are often provided in booklets or websites from funeral homes and crematoriums. Reviewing these choices and associated costs as fully as you can prior to the loss is as important as preparing for the end-of-life plan.

© 2009 barbara cameron pix

YES, DEATH IS BIG BUSINESS

FUNERAL OR CREMATION COST

When my sister Jody died, our family had a lot of decisions to make. What church? What funeral home? How do we get Jody's body moved? What casket? How many flowers and what kinds? The questions went on and on! What clothes should she be wearing? What cemetery will she be buried in? What tombstone? (In those days, cremation was less popular, so our family didn't even discuss it.)

Here are some financial ranges of costs you need to consider:

- For the *service*, which includes transportation, embalming, and funeral home staff, you can expect a bill of $1,400 to $3,600.
- The *casket* can cost from $700 to $10,000 depending on the style, design, and construction features.
- You can pay up to $5,000 or more for a *burial plot*, plus the maintenance fees and how you're going to mark the plot. Depending on the size of the *monument,* costs range from $400 to $1,200 or more. The costs for re-opening a family plot or vault runs $200 to $500.
- Oh, yes: the *flowers*. Prices can range from $175 to $400 and more, again depending on the choices the family makes.

To summarize all these expenses: you are looking at costs ranging from $7,775 to $10,410 (Statistics Canada reports the average Canadian spends $10,000 on a funeral).

For some Canadians, these funeral and burial costs, along with other considerations, have more of us turning to *cremation,* where the service can run under $2,000.

All of these financial considerations are complex, and at or around the time of death, are even more difficult to grasp and focus on. It would be an excellent idea to create a death plan ahead of time with clear heads and calm discussions, resulting in much better decisions being made for everyone. My mother and father-in-law have pre-arranged and pre-paid for their own funeral, allowing the entire family to devote their time and energy to each other and the good-byes.

Here are some questions you can use to help the entire family come to a clear understanding of what they can expect to pay for end-of-life care and funeral, burial, or cremation costs. This list will act as a useful catalyst to prompt further questions.

SOME QUESTIONS TO ASK THE ENTIRE FAMILY:

- What insurance coverage do we have in place? Does it include medical and relocation plans?
- What financial resources do we currently have to allocate to our loved one's care?
- What coverage should we arrange and can we afford it?
- Can we pre-plan and pre-pay for the funeral?
- What types of care facility should we consider? What costs are to be borne by the family?
- What medications will be necessary, and what portion will the family need to cover?
- What type of ceremony do we all intend to have?
- What are nice to haves and what are necessary ingredients?

- How much are we prepared and able to spend?
- Are there any associations, like Veteran Affairs that could provide some assistance?

Here is another piece of the puzzle. A friend of mine and I were talking about death and dying the other day and she sent along to me the "Five Wishes" document from VISTA Innovative Hospice Care. It is a simple set of questions that creates conversations helping families talk about what each person really wants. Here are the five questions:

1. Who do I want to make healthcare decisions for me when I can't?

2. How do I want to handle pain and to what level?

3. The kind of medical treatment I don't want is…

4. How do I want people, friends, family and professional staff to treat me?

5. What I want my loved ones to know is this…

I have created a workbook that can be found in the "Additional Resources" section at the end of this book. This booklet will help you collect and coordinate all the information you need to create a well-thought-through and heartfelt plan for yourself or a loved one.

"To the extent you are afraid to die, you're afraid to live."—John Penberthy

CHAPTER NINE

The Legacy—What am I Leaving Behind?

We have camped with the same group of people for thirteen years now. This weekend, however, I was shown how death has dignity. My friend Ron has inoperable terminal lung cancer—best guess from the doctors is that he's got until March 2012. Ron and his wife are heading to BC to spend some time with family, so they closed up the trailer for the season. We historically don't see Ron in the winter, so this was good-bye.Through tears, Ron spoke: "I have the easy job. I'm dying. The hard job is for the survivors; they are the ones that will carry the grief and the regret. So, have no regrets—just live!"—Neil Thrussell

What will others inherit from the way you lived your life? What will your personal legacy be? What will you leave behind?

As you age, you will ultimately come to a time in life when the years ahead are fewer than the years behind. Early in life it appears as though you have lots of time; there is no sense of the urgency that often comes with age—this is what bucket lists are all about! Look back at what you have done and fast-forward to what time is left. There is a natural and common urge for review and introspection.

- "What is it I really came here to do?"
- "What have I actually accomplished?"
- "How will people remember me?"
- "How would my family write my obituary? What do I really want it to say?"

These are the types of questions common to people as they consider their life and what they are leaving behind; in a very direct way they are making meaning of their life.

- "What was the point?"
- "Why was I here?"
- "Did I make a difference?"
- "Will anyone notice that I am gone?"
- "What can I do now that will help me feel complete in my life?"

After many conversations with elders over the years, I can attest to the fact that leaving a legacy behind is important to what it means to be human. Without a sense of creating something, you can lose meaning in your life. I know that the idea of a legacy may remind you of imminent death, and it is often impending death that brings up the topic, but it's not really about death at all.

This book, *When Death Speaks,* is all about your legacy; better still, it is about living a full, passionate, and purposeful life. Being reminded of death in this way is actually a good thing—it informs our lives. It gives us a perspective on what's important. Thinking about your legacy will help you decide the kind of life you want to live and the kind of world you want to create. No matter what your age or state of health, you will ultimately take stock of your accomplishments and disappointments, what you've done in the past, what you're doing now, and what you still hope to accomplish.

Many of us may not be a 'Bucky' Fuller or Lady Gaga, with our names and accomplishments being recognized worldwide. That doesn't reduce the need to create some meaning in our lives, to have what you've done and thought live on. Being practical, if you don't pass on your wisdom by leaving a legacy of some sort, the knowledge you've gained throughout the decades of your life, all the ups and all the downs, and all the insights will disappear as your physical body wears out and dies.

Your legacy can take many forms: children, grandchildren, a business, an ideal, a book, a community, or a home—something that has *you* in it. It makes sense that you would want to know how the world could remember you long after you're gone.

How can you identify your own legacy? What questions could you ask yourself or your closest friends and family members? How could you use your history to help discover your purpose? Here are some ideas and some focus questions that may help guide you in identifying your mission, your contribution, or as some would say, your gift.

USE YOUR OWN HISTORY

Any great book has what writers call a "through line", a theme that runs through the entire book. This through line is what all the chapters are linked to. It gives the book flow, and more importantly, meaning. Your life will have a theme to it, something that has consistently been there. You will see it in your work, your social life, your volunteer life, and likely your daydreams. It may even be a theme handed down from your father and perhaps even your grandfather.

Is there something that you often find yourself doing and enjoying? What is it?

As a child, did you have a dream you wanted to grow into? If yes, what was the dream? Did it happen? Can you start now?

Is there a similarity about your job(s), your hobbies, or your volunteer work? What is the commonality?

When I look back at my various jobs, volunteer positions, and passions, the common thread is people. In my banking career, it was about helping people and not so much about the money. In social services, it was much more obvious—helping people; my volunteer jobs were all serving the elderly. So the theme in my life is *serving and helping people.*

Go ahead and identify your own common thread or theme. Answer the questions I have posed, take some notes, do some journaling. Talk with close friends and family members and see what you can discover. Get curious about yourself; discover who you truly are and what you are doing.

ASK FAMILY AND FRIENDS

Many of your friends and family will have an outsider's view of who you are and what you are up to. They have a more objective perspective. Oftentimes you are so busy you don't really notice yourself or what you are consistently doing. By asking those close to you, the following questions may shed some light on what your personal mission is; it could be something so obvious that you don't even notice it.

- Do you notice something I do consistently in many areas of my life? What is it and why do you think this is so?
- When you think of me, what job would you say I am most suited for?
- What do you think I am trying to accomplish in my life?

Add the answers to these questions to your self-exploration and you will begin to see a theme emerge, a flow to your life, or a subtle yet deeper purpose. Take notes and compile a legacy journal for yourself.

WHO ARE YOUR HEROES?

Make a list. Why did you choose each of them?

You can learn lots about yourself by looking at your genuine heroes—men and women who have inspired you. Films you enjoy watching that tug on your heart are worth noticing too. What are the characters up to, and what are they doing that calls to your heart?

Is there a common set of values for all of them?

What were they each up to and did they have a similar purpose?

Add these observations to your legacy journal. Keep building the database, all the while looking for the theme that answers the question *What is it I came here to do?*

WHAT TURNS YOU ON?

What would have you leap from your bed a little earlier than normal and stay up a little later than usual? What do you work on that has time fly by? When do you feel the happiest in your day, week, or month?

For me, time flies when I am coaching people, staying in touch with friends and family, or writing. I notice that when I have spare time, I do one of three things; write an article, write my book, or contact friends and family. When I am sitting at the airport waiting for a flight, what do I notice myself doing? All of the above.

I usually have a notebook and pen with me—better still, my laptop. When an idea comes to me I jot it down. Sitting in the waiting room of the dentist's office, I will often find myself writing, usually articles that will help people deal with difficult personal issues. Getting curious about myself helps me see what I am up to.

What turns me on is writing about important life issues and being in touch with people in a supportive way!

WHAT ARE YOU LEAVING BEHIND?

ANOTHER REAL LIFE EXAMPLE

I remember meeting a most interesting fellow at the Seattle International Airport, terminal C. He ran a shoeshine business—a very *busy* shoeshine business! I noticed a line of people patiently waiting for their turn. It caught my attention, as it was a little unusual. I sat down on a bench across the hall and watched for a while.

Every one of his clients left his seat with a big smile on their face. I was intrigued and headed over for a shine. I sat down and introduced myself to Brian, and we began chatting like long-lost friends. Brian loved his business, especially his customers. You see, it was his purpose (legacy) to shine the hearts of his clients as he was shining their shoes (the excuse). Brian was known by all his clients, and also by others who worked near him, as the "heart shine guy"!

It got him up early in the morning with a smile on his face and a hop in his step. He was happy to shine the shoes of others; it helped him support his family, take care of his children, and put some money away for a rainy day. Brian was a man on a mission, having tremendous fun and living his legacy. He would be remembered as *the man who shined hearts.*

I was talking with a friend of mine from Calgary the other day. Steve and I love life and supporting others in living a full and passionate life. So of course the topic quickly came around to purpose and passion. Both of us being 'elders', we are keenly interested in legacy—what it is we are leaving behind. Here is some of what we spoke about; the rest of our conversation can be found on my website www.embraceyourdeath.com in the blog section under this title: Living from Death: The Story of Your Legacy.

I asked Steve what process he uses to support people in locating their deeper purpose or legacy. He replied, "It's very simple—here is what I say to them: first, sit quietly and take three deep breaths. Breathe in, extending your diaphragm, then breathe out while contracting your diaphragm; repeat this breath three times.

Now that you are even more present, list three key words that are nouns. They must have deep meaning for you—whether personally, or in your interactions with other people at work, at play, and socially. Write down these important words.

Next, identify three key actions you enjoy taking. That is, identify three action verbs ending in 'ing.' They could be verbs like *writing, creating, managing, playing* – these types of words. Write them down too."

"That sounds pretty simple," I chipped in. Steve nodded and continued without skipping a beat.

"Now go back to your three key or important words and define each word; flesh them out. What does each word mean to you? Develop a short story for each noun. The point is to really feel and understand the depth these three words carry for you.

Now the fun comes in," he said with a grin. "Take each action verb ending in 'ing' and link it to each important word you just finished describing. In total you will have written nine statements linking the action verb at the beginning of the statement with each of the nouns."

"Okay—this is not quite clear for me. Steve, can you give me an example or two?" I asked.

"Sure!" he said happily. "Creating community. *Writing about leadership. Managing teams. Making money.* These are all examples of an action verb linked to a noun. Here is the test of a great short phrase. If the statement you create sings to you, you tear up, and your gut flutters, you know your are on track with your heart. Take that two-word phrase and work with it until you settle on a statement of more than three words, and less than nine words."

"So let me clarify one point for your readers," Steve said. "If the short two-word phrase does not resonate with you, explore other verbs and important words. You will eventually find that meaningful connector of action and noun. The statement will ring true to you—that is, you will have a heartfelt response, and the phrase will become a personal mission statement, to coin a rather corporate analogy."

"Well, this all sounds great, Steve, and yet in a way I have heard this before. So what is it that will keep the readers on track with this legacy statement they have created?"

"You are right—this isn't New Age rocket science; this method has stood the test of time and is tried and true. What will keep us on track is this very simple and short formula:

The four simple actions I use to stay on track with my living legacy are:

1. Step up

2. Stay found

3. Share wisdom, and

4. Shine light"

"Sounds simple, my friend," I said. "Can you expand on those four phrases for me so I can really understand them?"

Steve jumped right in and continued by saying, "Sure! to *step up* means to communicate from commitment, from a place of meaning it. When listening and speaking, do so with integrity and from the courageous position of keeping your word—keep your promises. Stepping up means showing up, and it demonstrates how you have decided to live and lead.

To *stay found* means staying present—others may call it *presence.* Another way to say it is, when close to me, they experience my states of being spiritually, mentally, emotionally, and physically present. They get me as an alive human-being. Still with me?" Steve asked. As I nodded, he continued:

"To *share wisdom* means to share what you know—you teach. The adage 'When I listen, I learn, when I share I educate,' applies here."

"Finally, to *share light* means you light up (illuminate) what is in front of you. You remain joyfully grounded in business and busyness while having fun. You live a life of magnificence: you focus on what is magnificent and do so unabashedly."

"Alright, so we have guiding nouns and verbs, a guiding series of phrases, a three-to-nine words legacy statement, and a four-step formula so we can all stay on track. What's left?" I asked.

"My *21 Insights to Living Your Legacy*, of course," Steve beamed. "And here they are:

1. The experience of living your life is heightened when you educate others about living.

2. The legacy of living is passed on through your stories.

3. To stay honest in your living—'loving critics' are needed to give you feedback about what and how you are doing.

4. Knowing you are a role model is helpful in seeing yourself in the present.

5. In living with people, they need to know something about you—your hopes, dreams, talents, expectations, and loves.

6. Know thyself—know your value system.

7. Living is done in the open, with others. This is where you leave a legacy.

8. Trust is earned, and you have to keep working on trust as you live your legacy.

9. People commit to causes; a lasting living legacy is founded on your spoken principles and purpose.

10. You must decide on what matters in your life, before you can live a life that matters.

11. The words you choose to use matter.

12. Discover and share *your* true voice—be authentic in all of what you say.

13. Living is about forward thinking, having the intention through stories you share to engage others along the path.

14. In living, you notice what is going on around you *now*—use those insights.

15. The type of communication you use about living has intimacy, empathy and familiarity woven into the conversation.

16. Living is about making a difference; when taking a stand, it means being courageous.

17. Living is courage in action, guiding people to places they have not visited before, and where they cannot go without encouragement.

18. Failure is an option.

19. The legacy you leave is the life you lead.

20. Answer the question 'Who am I being?' with each breath, with each action!

21. Below is the last insight in the form of a question. You must keep asking and answering this question daily—it informs your legacy statement today and every day in living from your obituary:

22. For your legacy to be more than well-written words, what needs to be true in your life today?"

A heart felt thank you to my friend and colleague Steven Hobbs. Google him and check out his website—he is an inspiring elder!

So let me close this section by asking a question or two. What will get you up early in the morning with a smile on your face? What will keep you up late at night? What will have you make that extra effort to go the extra mile? Go ahead, work through this chapter, answer all the questions it contains. Keep track of your answers and see where they all lead. Once you've had a look at what you've come up with, write your own personal mission statement. Here is mine:

"With love, authenticity, compassion, and humor, I intend to change the conversation Canadians have about death from one of denial and fear to one of embrace and inspiration."

Once your legacy work is complete, all that is left to do is line your life up with what it is you intend to leave behind. This is where the magic and joy lie! Have fun with it, be the creator of your own universe. I can't wait to see your obituary!

A human being is part of a whole, called by us a universe, a part limited in time and space. He experiences himself, his thoughts and feelings, as something separated from the rest, a kind of optical delusion of his consciousness. —Albert Einstein – 1950

CHAPTER TEN

And in the End—Creating your own Celebration of Life

Death is by no means separate from life...We all interact with death every day, tasting it as we might a wine, feeling its keen edge even in trifling losses and disappointments, holding it by the hand, as a dancer might a partner, in every separation. We pump the soul into every mystery from within, from inside our own experience.— Eugene Kennedy

---

I was talking with my financial planner the other day when it came to me that some people might plan for the logistics of their death, such as wills, life insurance and all that important stuff. Some may plan for where they want to be buried or where their ashes are to be spread. Others may choose the music they want played at their funeral. Most of us, though, don't plan at all, because the conversation is just too darn tough to have. As a matter of fact, over 80 percent of Canadians do not have this part of their life planned at all! These statistics were revealed in two recent studies, one by Ipsos-Reid, and a second in a national study of the elderly.

In this chapter, let us look at the idea of planning a great celebration for the life we and loved ones lived as best as we could! Let's look at ways to include the one who is dying, if that is desired by them and if it is possible, especially if she or he has already expressed their wishes.

If you were to plan your living funeral how would it look?

We have event planners, wedding planners, birth planners, financial planners, city planers, and community planners—why would we not have death planners? Here are a few more questions you can ask yourself or a loved one:

- What would the theme of the celebration be?
- How would you record it?
- When would it be held?
- Who would be the host?
- Would there be food and drink?
- Who would handle it?

CREATE YOUR OWN CELEBRATION OF LIFE

All the above questions can be used to prepare gracefully and lovingly for the end of life.

The other day I read a great article written by Maris Beck in May 2011. It came all the way from Australia. It certainly shines a different light on the topic of creating life celebrations and ways of taking care of the body of your loved ones. Have a look, and we will continue our discussion once you've read it.

"When Peter Macfarlane's father lay dying, he had the urge to climb into bed with him and hold him close. Death was about relationships and memories.

Now, the architect and RMIT doctoral student is using his skills to humanize one of the traditions of death. He is re-inventing the tombstone—so hard and angular it 'pushes you away'—to create spaces for contemplation and connection with the memory of the deceased.

He made a baby's tombstone that was designed to look like a womb. It was a circular monument lined with wood, and family members could sit inside it. It had a tiny hole, where sunlight would shine through for one minute every year, in honor of the moment of the baby's birth.

Death, it seems, is having a makeover.

Interest in the environment is changing funerals, too, and some dying people are choosing to hold "living funerals" before they pass away.

PhD student Pia Interlandi has designed death shrouds with biodegradable fabric.

Some of the shrouds are embroidered with synthetic threads so that when the fabric decomposes, the embroidered patterns are left behind. She hopes people will choose patterns they want to wear for eternity, such as the pattern of their family tree.

Ms Interlandi, who has dressed several relatives before their burial, says wrapping the body is a valuable part of mourning that has been overlooked in modern funerals. It helps people realize that the soul of their loved one is truly gone, she says. She believes that as people become more aware of conserving natural resources, they may stop using coffins altogether in favor of the funeral shroud.

''Green burials' are increasingly popular. At Lilydale Memorial Park in Victoria, there are no headstones. The cemetery uses GPS to mark the graves so 'there are no traditional headstones to mar the natural beauty of the grounds''.

Several Australian companies make coffins out of recycled cardboard, which can be airbrushed with colorful designs.

Green funerals are still fairly rare, the general manager of Tobin Brothers Funeral Directors, James McLeod, says, but even mainstream funerals have changed from twenty years ago.

''In funerals today, there is more focus on celebrating the life rather than mourning.'

Even before death, things are changing. A handful of people are celebrating their life with friends and family before they die in 'living funerals'. The director of Living Wakes, Philip Holland, almost lost the chance to tell his own father how much he loved him. With his father in a coma, Mr. Holland and his family began discussing turning off life support. But his father woke up, and Mr. Holland says he started Living Wakes after realizing how important it was to pay respect to people before they die.

'So often I've been to funerals where people say, *Oh, he would have loved this*, and I thought, *wouldn't it be nice if he were here?* It's not about grieving at all; it's about telling that person how you feel about them before you lose the opportunity.'

Rodney Syme, a noted advocate of dying with dignity, plans to have a living funeral when he senses his own death is imminent. He says he will invite friends and family and say: 'This is who I am, this is what I've done, you are my friends. Let's celebrate my life … I regard that as a good death.'

But the Victorian director of the National Funeral Directors Association, Malcolm Dubock, says most people still choose traditional ceremonies. 'I think they go back to the security of the past. They go back to what their mothers did and what their fathers did.'''

I put a copy of this article into the book to give you permission to allow yourself to create an end-of-life celebration that would be unique for you, your loved ones, and the one who has died.

When death is knocking, I hope there will be time to gather family and friends around, have a BBQ, play some cribbage, tell some silly jokes, likely drink a rum and coke or two, and really enjoy each other's company. I want the gathering to be just that—a fun event, an opportunity for us all to remember great times we had in life together. And, I want to be a part of it, a living funeral if you will.

And yes, I will play some of my favorite music: the Beatles, Rolling Stones, k.d. lang and some Leonard Cohen, perhaps some Men at Work, music that will drive my wife, and my boys a little crazy! I fully intend to have a grand celebration of my life, relationships, and accomplishments before I kick the bucket!

When I am dead I want relatives and close friends around to support my core family members. I would like, all things being equal, my body to be handled, washed and dressed by my close family. At the crematorium I want the environment to be celebratory and fun. After all, it is only my body that is gone. I want my ashes to be placed in an urn.

Sonora and I loved our travels in India and I particularly loved Varanasi. So I want to be taken by my wife to my favorite of all Indian cities. Then at dawn, walk me down to the Ghats, rent a boat and take me out onto the Ganges rivers and spread me far and wide.

This is my wish for a great death: celebrate with loved ones before I go; go quietly when I die; and have a great trip to my favorite place as a last good-bye. Depending on the finances, it could also be as simple as taking my ashes to favorite provincial park, Caren Range Park, and spread my ashes at the base of the first-growth cedars, or spreading them around a rose bush in the home garden.

Although talking about death in this way has been unthinkable for decades, it is time to bring discussions like these to the family room, or kitchen table. How would you like to create a celebration of a life lived by a loved one? What kind of fond memories and memorabilia would you like to have at the ceremony? How would you like all the guests to remember the deceased?

Golf clubs and playing cards and a cribbage board were by my Dad's casket!

What sort of treasures could you create to pass along to family members as a keepsake? These days with all this social media stuff you could use a Facebook page as a gathering place for well wishes and blessings. The only limit to the celebration is your own imagination.

Here are some basic steps you can take that will ensure the creative planning you have done has a great chance of being realized.

Learn about medical interventions. What are your quality-of-life bottom lines? Will that mean staying in hospital? Will being unable to communicate be acceptable to you? What are some pain treatments and what are their side effects? Remember, you can receive comfort care even if you refuse aggressive treatment.

Think about how you want your death to be. Who you would want present? Once in a hospice or hospital palliative care, would you want music? Are you worried about pain and or the loss of control? Talk with your doctor and get clear regarding what options are possible.

With good medical care you can live well until the moment you die.

Make Notes. Some experts recommend specifying medical interventions you'd like. Others say that because no one can predict the nature of their death, it is better to record what you value in life such as being pain-free. Some professionals encourage you not to use terms such as 'no heroic measures,' which can be unclear. *Legal documents such as a living will or personal care directives are important to have in place.* Remember to be clear and precise.

Tell your loved ones about your wishes. Appoint an alternate decision-maker, a family member or good friend. Make sure they know about your living will, power of attorney, care directives, and organ donor registration. Remember to let your entire family know who you have appointed as your alternate decision-maker so as to be clear and avoid confusion.

Revisit your plans often. Although it is best to have it, your care plan does not need a lawyer's signature, so you can update it regularly, say once each year. You can always keep a copy in your wallet, where emergency room or medical staff would find it and consider it as part of your care. Remember to have a copy at home and let your family know where you have it filed.

There you have it: several stories about how creative you can get in planning both a living funeral and your final funeral. Take this chapter of the book as your permission to create a death celebration worth living for! At the end of the book in the "Additional Resources" section you will find a mini-planning workbook called" Celebrating A Life: A Planning and Organizing Workbook". It is designed to help you prepare the gathering and handle all the necessary details.

Death? Why this fuss about death. Use your imagination, try to visualize a world without death! ... Death is the essential condition of life, not an evil.—Charlotte Perkins Gilman

END NOTES

THERE IS LIGHT AFTER THE STORM

Although this book is entitled **When Death Speaks** it is the new lease on life that is important. After all, it is your loved one that is dead; you, the survivor remain. What are the lessons you can learn from your loved one's passing? How can their parting or your imminent death help you to live an inspired life from now on? What lessons can you learn from the deathbed that will help you lead a more full and passionate life now? When facing your own death how can its certainty inspire you to live as fully as you can each day you are alive?

In nature, where there is darkness, somewhere else there is light. When there is birth, somewhere else there is a death. Nature exists in pairs; all we need to do is look for the opposite. So there is a death—where is there new life? There is an end to a relationship— where is the beginning of a new one?

Let us not be blinded by death in the future, in the present, or in the past. Death can be a key that opens a door to life anew. Death can be a tremendous inspiration to your work and career, to your family, and to all your relationships. You can be moved to do spontaneous and loving things, given that death is inevitable—only the timing is uncertain. Do we really have tomorrow to wait for?

I can tell you that the fact that people don't talk about it makes it a whole lot worse.—Kate Evans

ADDITIONAL RESOURCES

Shakespeare summed it up well:

> *Who would Fardels bear,*
> *To grunt and sweat under a weary life,*
> *But that the dread of something after death,*
> *The undiscovered Country, from whose bourn*
> *No traveller returns, puzzles the will,*
> *And makes us rather bear those ills we have,*
> *Than fly to others that we know not of.*
> *Thus Conscience does make Cowards of us all.*

In this section of the book you will find helpful basic guides that will support you in your desire to create a great life celebration, a well-considered and detailed death plan, a fuller understanding about death and grief, and a deeper appreciation for life.

Due to its somewhat limited occurrence, and yet its profoundly unique impact on families and friends, I have included a full study on suicide in this section of the book. This piece was carefully researched and compassionately written by my friend and colleague Reuben. I have placed it here for much the same reason as the pieces on grief and children, and women and miscarriages—because of the unique impact on the individuals surviving it.

Here are the resources included in this section:
- A Celebration of Life, Planning and Organizing
- Preparing for Death, a Practical Check List
- Kids and Death, Some Helpful Hints for Adults
- An Exploration into the Nature of Suicide by Reuben Weinstangel
- Miscarriage, Abortion, and Infertility—The Invisible Death

IT'S OKAY TO FEEL JOY IN THE MIDST OF THE STORM

A CELEBRATION OF LIFE
PLANNING & ORGANIZING

In taking the step to create your own living funeral there is much to consider and plan for. I created this basic mini-workbook to provide a framework for the important family discussion that needs to take place for the event to be both a personal expression of life and a successful, joyful, celebration.

The workbook is divided into two sections. The first is a series of questions that will lead to the open conversations that need to happen to flesh out exactly what the loved one and the family want to create. There are also questions designed to help the planners assess issues like finances, date, location, time, and length of celebration, given current health-related considerations. At the end of this first section is a recap that draws together on one sheet of paper the key words and phrases that will help focus your planning.

The second section helps the planning group organize the tasks that need to be handled into categories, people responsible for the task, and a timeline to complete the jobs.

The final page is a checklist that will assist the planner to gracefully and simply organize the event with as little stress as possible. Remember, you are creating a celebration, so do your best to have lots of fun with it!

SECTION ONE – LIFE CELEBRATION QUESTIONS
THE IDEAL CELEBRATION

This portion of the workbook is the daydream piece where the individual and their family can have fun planning the party. Don't rule anything out! I would have a big piece of paper taped on the wall and simply write down *all* the ideas the family has about creating a celebration of a lifetime!

It's called a brainstorming session. It works best when the ideas are simply written down as they pop out. It has been discovered that if you start checking each idea out, making comments about its workability, etc, the creative juices will slow down and people may hold back their more unique ideas and likely get bored. So leave the workability conversation for a little later; simply enjoy the fun of being creative and perhaps a little wild and crazy!

You might want to hand everyone post-it notes so they could write down their ideas and simply stick them on the larger flip chart paper. This way those shy family members can contribute too, and not feel the pressure of having to speak out loud in front of people. If you use this process, then all you need to do is group the ideas on the post-it notes into themes or categories.

Here are some general questions you can use to guide the creative session:
- What are your favorite foods and drinks?
- Who would you love to have there? Friends, family, bosses, employees, doctor, nurses or priest?
- Where do you want to have it?
- What kind of feeling(s) do you want people to leave with?
- What favorite music would you love to share with your friends and family?
- What is theme do you want to create? Decorations?
- Are there any special things you want to have at the celebration? Favorite car, pictures, books, clothes, games, musical instruments?
- How do you want to 'remember' this gathering? Audio, video, pictures, autograph book?

Simply record the thoughts and ideas.

Once you have exhausted everyone's creative ideas, do a recap by reviewing the items. This review will often reignite people's creative energy and you may find a few more new ideas coming out. Record the new ideas and include them too!

Great—you have created your ideal celebration or wish list. Set it aside for now and we will come back to it shortly.

PRACTICAL, LOGISTICAL, AND HEALTH CONCERNS

Now comes the time to look at and review the practical matters. Here is a checklist of key considerations you must mull over as you decide on what can be created for your loved one's living funeral:

X The person's level of health and physical ability
X The medical prognosis
X Necessary medical support
X Their place of living
X The event timing
X Money
X Food and beverages
X Number of guests

Putting on your practical hat, it is now time to go through the reality of the situation and consider what is possible given these logistical and medical considerations.

Once you have compiled the list of practical and health considerations, go back to the creative ideas you compiled during your brainstorming fun. Simply take each idea and screen it through the considerations and concerns you came up with.

RECAP OF KEY WORDS AND PHRASES

Now that you have the creative ideas sorted out and they are balanced against real-life considerations, you can make a list of key words and phrases that will be the guiding principles or themes of the event. Here are examples:

Fun, humorous, and carefree.
A joyful walk down memory lane.
A happy celebration with all of Dad's important stuff.
Great food, amazing friends, and Mom's favorite music.

These words and phrases can lead directly into a vision or mission statement to guide you forward towards your goals. So go ahead and create a celebration statement that will guide you and all the family and friends in creating a life celebration to live for!

Here are a couple of examples of a life celebration vision statement that will help you understand what I mean:

To remember Dad in a fun and humorous way
with lots of friends and family having the time of their life.
Let's have the happiest, craziest party ever so we can all remember
how much Mom loves to have great times with company.

SECTION TWO – LIFE CELEBRATION TASK LIST

© 2010 barbara cameron pix

THE BIGGEST GIFT YOU CAN GIVE TO YOUR FAMILY
IS BEING PREPARED FOR YOUR DEATH

The table below is an example of how you can break down all the items on the list into manageable categories and tasks. I have put a couple of entries under each heading as examples for you. Some areas might have lots of tasks; others may have only one. Either way, this is a fine method to organize all the details so that the celebration happens as you have planned it, give or take the usual oops!

By organizing the event you can also see how important it is to assign dates so that tasks are completed on time. It helps you see when a friend or family member has too many tasks to do and gives a hint when you could ask for a bit more help, or simplify things.

The Task	The Person	The Budget	By When	Date Completed
Food and Drinks				
Call caterer	Susan	$500.00	Oct. 1/2011	
Purchase liquor	Harry	$500.00	Oct. 15/2011	
Decorations				
Hawaiian Items	Marge	$100.00	Oct. 15/2011	
Artificial palm trees	Marge	$50.00	Oct. 15/2011	
Music				
Sound System	Bill	His own	Oct. 15/2011	

CDs and iPod playlist	Hillary	Her own	Oct. 8/2011
Guest Invites			
Handle invitations	George	$100.00	Sept. 15/2011
Make phone calls	Peter	n/a	Sept. 15/2011
Location			
Family Home	n/a	n/a	Oct. 22/2011
Memorabilia			
Dad's crib board			
Dad's golf clubs			
Picture Board			
Thank you notes			
Family task	All of us	$100.00	Nov. 15/2011
Photos and Taping	Alex	n/a	Oct. 22/2011

PREPARING FOR DEATH
A PRACTICAL CHECKLIST

Professor Udo Schuklenk, a philosopher from Queen's University, and his team of researchers were reviewing the end-of-life issues for a study published in the fall of 2011. There were many interesting issues brought to light, some which really demonstrated how poorly prepared many people are when it comes to death.

Though it is clear that most Canadians want to die at home, more than 70 percent of us die in a hospital and often in a special care unit. This is partly attributable to the fact that less than 25 percent of us have advanced directives or a living will prepared. Our fear of death precipitates our unconscious aversion to getting our final care issues in order well in advance of the event. This workbook will walk you through the many basic details that need to be handled in order that you and your loved ones can relax fully into your life knowing that all the important and necessary details have been handled as you would want them to be.

This handbook is broken down into six sections: family, key information, legal, financial, physical and health information, and digital information. At the end of the Key Information section is an easy to follow To Do List that will help ensure all of the important issues are handled. Though many sections may overlap to a degree, it is important to take note of the important areas of life that need to be managed in order that all details are well-planned and can be more easily handled at the time of death.

Whether the death is expected or sudden, it's a time of overwhelming emotions. Families can find themselves making poor and/or costly decisions for both the loved one dying and for themselves.

Having all the information you need easily at hand, you will make the arrangements and move forward much more efficiently. Completing all these forms in advance, reviewing and updating them will provide certainty that the folks handling all the arrangements haven't dropped out any details. It will also reduce the feelings of being overwhelmed that are all too common.

I would recommend creating a binder that will contain all the organized information. Keep a copy for yourself, put one in a safety deposit box and a third with your lawyer so it can be easily found and referred to when needed. For those of you living in Canada, there is a helpful publication entitled Compassionate Care Benefits available through Service Canada that can be added to your binder.

KEY INFORMATION

Personal Data
Name:
Date and place of birth:
Address:
Telephone number:
Father and mother's names and places of birth:
Occupation:
Spouse's name:
Date and place of birth:
Address:
Telephone number:
Father and mother's names and places of birth:
Occupation:

FAMILY INFORMATION

Family of Origin Data
Grandparents, aunts and uncles
Next of Kin
Children
Grandchildren
Physician & Health Information
Doctor's name and contact information
Specialist(s) name and contact information
Care or Senior's Home information
Medical insurance card number

Organ donor certificate
Current medical conditions
Cemetery plot—prearranged and prepaid?
Funeral arrangements—prearranged and prepaid?
Legal Information
Lawyer's name and contact information
(Location of important papers)

	Home	Deposit Box	Lawyer
Will			
Living Will			
Power of Attorney			
Property Deed			
Property Insurance			
Mortgage Papers			
Birth Certificate			
Marriage Certificate			
Automobile Registration & Insurance			
Insurance Policies			

Financial Information
Banking Institution and accounts
Life Insurance Company
Safety Deposit Box and signees
Credit Cards
Investment contacts
Real Estate
Pensions and company contacts
Tax Returns
Organizations
Business and Community Associations
Digital Information
Email account(s) and passwords
Subscription website(s) and passwords
Social media site(s) and passwords

TO DO LIST

Documents to Gather
- Will, Living Will, Power of Attorney and Enduring Power of Attorney
- Birth certificate
- Passport or citizenship papers
- Social Insurance Number
- Marriage Certificate
- Insurance policies
- Bank Statements
- Car registration and insurance
- Property deeds and mortgage papers
- Income tax return previous year
- Disability claims
- Pension information

Decisions to make promptly
- Cemetery or cremation location – death certificate
- Funeral home or crematorium
- Where to hold the service
- Time of service and funeral or cremation
- Meeting with funeral/crematorium director and clergy, regarding details
- Type of memorial and inscription
- Casket or urn
- Clothing for deceased if necessary
- Type of service
- Clergy or person to officiate
- Charitable foundation for gifts in memory
- Information for obituary and eulogy
- Choosing the pall-bearers
- Flowers
- Home preparations for family and guests
- Childcare for children
- Transportation
- Completing necessary documentation
- Managing all calls and cards
- Check will for special requests

People to notify quickly
- Relatives
- Doctor (if not present)
- Employer
- Lawyer

- Executor
- Insurance companies
- Cemetery
- Friends
- Pallbearers
- Church and community organizations
- Newspaper

Things to pay (for if not already prepaid)

- Cemetery plot
- Funeral ceremony or cremation service
- Memorials
- Priest or minister
- Florist
- Medical costs
- Hospital and ambulance
- Death Certificate
- Lawyers
- Current bills including:
  - Internet and telephone
  - Unpaid medical bills
  - Mortgage or rent
  - Gas or hydro
  - Insurance premiums
  - Installment payments
  - Income Taxes payable

KIDS AND DEATH

Some Helpful Hints for Adults

© 2006 barbara cameron pix

LET YOUR CHILDREN KNOW THAT GRIEF IS A JOURNEY YOU CAN TAKE TOGETHER

When I was young, eleven years old, I think, my Grandpa Joe died. I knew he was in the hospital and wasn't really well, yet that was all I knew—until one day my folks told me Grandpa was no longer with us and we would be going to the funeral on the weekend. You may wish to review what I have shared at the opening of this book.

Adults tried to reassure me, and yet their unwillingness to answer my questions did exactly the opposite. Just because I was a kid didn't mean I couldn't understand. I sure felt a lot, and I just needed someone to talk with me about what I was feeling and why I was confused; I needed an adult to talk with me openly and truthfully in a way I could understand.

This handbook will give you hints about kids and death in short easy-to-read points, much the way you could talk with children about death. You will notice I don't mince words—I write shorter sentences and in language children would use. I talk with the children in their world, and in their language so they can understand and make sense of their feelings, what they see and what they hear, in order to ensure all the messages are congruent.

As adults, it is our responsibility to teach children, our own and others, how to deal with the loss of a loved one. Showing them how to be open, honest, and loving while experiencing a painful loss will help children learn about both the joy and the pain that results from loving family and friends deeply. It will help them embrace fully both life and death.

It is also important to understand the different levels of development our kids grow through. This mini-handbook will deal with two categories: teenagers and younger children. There are many wonderful books on grief and children. This section provides a brief look at the basic and important factors to understand about your kids as they grieve.

GENERAL GUIDELINES

Trust your heart, your own intuition, and feeling senses. From this perspective, encourage the truth to be told gently yet honestly. Children are great at sensing when adults are being over-protective and when adults are denying the truth themselves.

Do your best to use appropriate words such as death, dead, and died. Trying to soften the impact by using words like "Grandpa is resting" will only confuse the child. Help the child learn that not talking about it will not make it go away.

Find a creative way to let the children know that grief is a process or a journey. Use examples that children can understand to help them see that they can get through the feelings. Let them know it is fine to express their feelings, as it is also fine for you to express yours.

Younger children are not able to process the intensity of adult emotions through their bodies, so they do it in bits and pieces. They may be sad for a moment and then run off happily playing. It is fine that they do this, and let them know that having fun and playing does not mean they don't miss or care about their loved one. Kids also move around a lot more than adults, so don't take their activity as a sign of disrespect; sometimes children just need to move.

Children need someone to talk to about death, just as adults do. Keep their conversations with you confidential, unless of course the child's safety is at risk, or they are behaving in unusual and abnormal ways and other parents need to know.

Watch for the quiet child who seems all right and yet isn't expressive at all. They may need support too, even though their grief isn't as obvious as it is with a child who is much more extroverted.

COMMON MYTHS ABOUT CHILDREN AND GRIEF

Myth: *Children don't feel the same way adults do when grieving.* Well, of course they don't. Every person grieves in their own unique way, given their developmental level, background, family of origin and culture. It is normal and healthy that we each express our grief in our own 'style'.

Myth: *I must protect my child from the pain of the loss.* This myth gets tied in with thoughts like *they are too young, they wouldn't understand, I might upset them if I talk about it, taking part in the funeral would upset them too much, I won't know the right thing to say, they don't want to talk about it anyway.* All these thoughts are not helpful, and may just be the adult avoiding a painful situation. Kids know and understand a lot more than we adults give them credit for. Children feel deeply too, and need to be taught how to express their emotions in a healthy way. By talking about the loss, whether you say the right thing or not, you are also acknowledging the child's grief. Excluding them from the funeral or ceremonies will oftentimes be even more upsetting for the children. They know when upset is present and when it is being hidden.

Myth: *Don't say death, died or dying they're too harsh. Use words like gone away, went to heaven, or is resting.* All these terms adults use to soften the blow will actually confuse the kids. Grandpa is gone will likely be followed by a question like "Where?" *Mother's gone to a better place* could be questioned like this: "Can we got there too?" It is much more helpful to tell it like it is. "Grandpa is dead," is a much better approach. It is real, and this is what the child needs to learn to handle with your loving support and directness. Refrain from going overboard, though, telling the children all the facts all at once. This can be very overwhelming for any one especially a young child.

Myth: *Talking about, looking at or touching the body is not right.* Quite to the contrary—it is very normal for children to push and poke and touch. Teach them how to do this respectfully ,and let them feel the body if they wish. They will notice the person is not really there. It will help them know that death is real and also help them say goodbye.

SOME HELPFUL HINTS

Children are going to go through lots of emotions and different phases as they grieve and mourn the loss. They may go through a phase where they are full of sadness, hopelessness, and despair. They may really deny the death and will possibly protest it, hoping if they do that things will go back to normal. The child may have challenges concentrating both at home and at school.

Ultimately the child will begin to put their life back together without the loved one she or he just lost. As they do this they are beginning to accept the death. They will need to find their own way to have the death make sense to them in their understanding of life.

Helping your child move through these stages or phases of their own unique journey of grief will prepare them well for the ups and downs of life ,and will also give them confidence that they can get through losses no matter how painful they may be. This will also give your child confidence that people can help them as they go through life.

What you can do to support your child is help them tell their story of the death as it is for them. Teach them new words and phrases to help them understand and accept the loss. Let them know that their feelings are okay, and help your child express them in a healthy way. Show them by example and simply listen.

Know also that it may take many repetitions to help the child understand what has happened. They too may need to repeat the story often to 'get it'. They may also say things that sound weird to you as an adult; things that they just blurt out like "It is all my fault." They may not really believe it and may change it moments later as they explore their feelings and emotions.

Help your children to remember the loved one they lost by cherishing keepsakes, having little ceremonies, or telling stories or drawing pictures. Help them to finish any leftover business with their loved one; Saying goodbye, telling their loved one how much they will miss them, or, saying I love you.

Watch for areas of confusion, things your child doesn't understand, and then simply help them straighten out the misunderstanding. Listen to them and support them through the expression of their feelings and emotions. Teach them how to express and understand the more challenging emotions like guilt and anger.

Importantly, don't wait until the family has experienced a loss to explain death and dying to your child. At times of loss ,emotions are already overwhelming for everyone, including the children. So make time when family life is 'normal' to have conversations with them about death, loss, love, and life. By having these rituals and chats you normalize life and death, and love and loss with your kids. You will actually build your relationship with your kids by having these talks, letting them know that your family can have the difficult conversations and grow from them. Remember, you can also contact you local hospice society for support.

I was in Burlington, Ontario at the Bay Centre Funeral Homes presenting a talk on "Embrace Your Death" in the fall of 2011. It was a fun evening, full of great information, wonderful conversations, and many new acquaintances. One such new friendship was with Jane George, author of *Playing With the Angels: Stories of Possibilities for Grieving Children*. She approached me after my talk with a warm smile and wonderful hug. She offered me a copy of her book as a gift for my uplifting talk about death and grief. We chatted briefly and off she went.

I read through her book the next day and was taken with her approach to grief for kids. It is an amazing book and really does address the children where they are, at their level, mentally, spiritually, and emotionally. It feels as if she were a child as she wrote the book. It speaks directly to children in a way that they will understand. The book lovingly addresses all the kinds of things adults might say to make children feel better, but in fact only confuse the issue. It talks about all the emotional things that could go on for kids.

I encourage you to get a copy of this wonderful book; it is very helpful! It also supports much of what I have written in this small but important section of children and grief.

© 2012 barbara cameron pix

SUICIDE CAN BE THE LONELIEST DEATH OF ALL

AN EXPLORATION INTO THE NATURE OF SUICIDE

by Reben Weinstangel

Shortly after I graduated from university, I was offered a position working at a suicide research clinic in Montreal, Quebec. This was an exciting time as I was filled with a loving readiness to help and an eagerness to learn. The prospect of leaving a positive impact in the lives of others brightened my days, even when the environment was emotionally charged and turbulent. But, as it turns out, the experience at this clinic was going to be wholly unique in its opportunities for me, as my clients were already dead.

My job was to run psychological autopsies through a series of systematized investigations. This is the method by which information is retrospectively gathered about a person's death. The goal is to reconstruct what the person thought, felt, and did before they died, as well as to determine if any psychological diagnoses were missed while the person was still alive. This type of case analysis is based on information gathered from both documentation and face-to-face interviews with family, friends, and others who were close to the deceased.

As for the source of these documents, some were confidential medical histories sent to us from various hospitals and psychological clinics. We also received reports from the coroner's office and other various institutions connected with the case. Family members and friends provided other relevant personal effects. Occasionally, we would find other sources through our own investigations. We had suicide notes, journals, psychological examinations, school and police records, correspondences, and whatever else we could get our hands on to paint a more accurate picture of the person.

The training was extensive as we learned how to conduct various diagnostic interviews. We learned what questions to ask and how to ask them to get the information that we needed. We were also taught how to conduct psychological analyses of our suicide victims. As the weeks went on, the team and I became increasingly adept at isolating and clustering symptoms into various diagnoses.

By the time that the training was done we were all ready to go speak to the people who were closest to the victims. However, opportunities to head out were rare and distributed in order of seniority. I had to wait for my turn, but as luck would have it, this turned out to be a blessing in disguise.

Over the years, the massive file cabinets had become disorganized with hundreds of muddled case files. I was appointed the arduous task of putting them back in order, reanalyzing each one in case something was missed. As it turns out, this was more fascinating than I ever could have hoped.

Inside each manila folder was a story, and I needed to determine the buildup and conditions that caused the main character to die. Each person had a different set of circumstances that they faced. They had different familial histories, psychological profiles, social and environmental living conditions, socio-economic statuses, medical histories, age groups, genders, and an array of other distinguishing features. Each new element made the analyses more complex and unique.

In as many ways as the people differed in the circumstances that led to their decision, so too did they differ in their views regarding life and death. Some were practicing members of religious communities, while others were atheists and agnostic in belief. Others described their philosophical and existential views of the world at length in their suicide notes and journals.

As the weeks progressed, each new profile went from being a static and lifeless collection of documents to becoming real people again in the mind of a stranger sitting in a backroom office in a gloomy hospital. With each new story, I was faced with my own deliberations about our right to die and views regarding suicide. My goal in this chapter is simply to share with you my impressions of what I have learned and experienced.

For the purposes of this exploration, I am going to suspend any personal judgments on the actions of the victims involved. Also, out of respect for the victims and families, I've changed the names of the people involved and some of details of their stories. These vignettes are a tribute to the people who chose to die and to their families and friends who were welcoming and kind to us as we searched for answers.

THE STORY OF ERIC

Eric was thirty-seven years old and had just recently separated from his wife, Sarah. They were married for six years but had been fighting regularly for the last two. During the last six months of their marriage he found himself alone most nights, not knowing where she was. Sarah eventually admitted that she was having an affair with his best friend, Steven, and that she wanted a divorce.

Over the next few weeks, Eric emotionally spiraled as his life unraveled. He quit his job, began drinking heavily, and pined over a relationship that he refused to accept was over. Steven refused to explain himself or take responsibility for what he had done. Sarah stopped accepting his calls. This did not stop Eric from trying to contact her. Each failed attempt magnified his feelings of desperation as he tried to win her back.

His friends and family tried to help but there was little they could do to mediate the situation. Most of his friends were also her friends and many refused to get involved. He condemned them for this and pushed them away. He closed down his world to everybody except the one person who had rejected him.

He obsessed over the situation, overwhelmed by the interpersonal discord, his financial issues, resulting from his unemployment, and his upcoming legal battle with Sarah. We coded for major depression and generalized anxiety disorder in the months leading up to his death. He was self-medicating with alcohol and refused to go seek professional help. He felt abandoned, betrayed, socially rejected and isolated, worthless, and hopeless about the future.

Eric internalized the actions of those around him as a direct reflection of his self-worth. He felt defective and undeserving of a second chance. He characterized himself as a burden to her and wondered how he could be so selfish by sabotaging her newfound happiness.

His last day was spent drinking alone in his apartment. He addressed his suicide note directly to Sarah. The extent of his intoxication at the time of writing was obvious at first glance. In it he apologized to her for failing to be the man that she needed him to be. He expressed his torment regarding the state of his life and explained that he cannot bear the thought of being a burden to her any longer. He ended the note by saying that he loved her and that he hoped she could forgive him for what he was about to do. He was found a couple of days later when his family was unable to reach him and went to his apartment. The toxicology report stated that he had died from a combination of alcohol poisoning and an overdose on various painkillers.

DISCUSSION

Divorce can feel like a death and it may be tempting to say that Eric had been driven mad by a lovelorn heart. This is part of a commonly romanticized myth of Romeo and Juliet style suicides. In this scenario, a young lover is unable to cope with the recent loss of a partner and impulsively ends his or her own life as a result. While we know that impulsivity in male youth is a risk factor for suicide, it is important to realize that these types of deaths are rarely seen. It is far more likely that Eric's suicidal behavior was multi-determined, resulting from a longstanding series of maladaptive coping strategies and an escalating sequence of responses to stressful life events.

We also know from reports in his file that Eric had experienced a run of hardships during his childhood and adolescence. He had spent some time in a group home during his parent's separation. His grandfather, who was his primary father figure at the time, died shortly thereafter. Eric began drinking and had developed an addiction to ketamine as a way of dealing with his loss.

His relationship with his family remained poor throughout his life. They rarely expressed care for one another, were not very connected as a unit, and found themselves in frequent, and sometimes even violent, arguments. His mother suffered from major depressive episodes and was inconsistent in her levels of affection towards him and his siblings. His sister reported how quickly their mother would teeter back and forth between praise and condemnation. In line with this kind of history, Eric suffered from severe long-term interpersonal difficulties with the people around him.

Having stable social networks in our lives can help us to mitigate the affects of negative emotional impacts. They act as a protective factor that can help buffer us from feeling the full-effects of disparaging life events. We rely on each other for love and support. For these reasons, unrequited love and the disruption of interpersonal relationships are prevalent risk factors for suicide.

Sometimes, this disconnect is forced upon a person. In these times, it is even more critical that we seek out new connections to help us rebuild. Unfortunately, one of the ironies of depression and suicidality is the tendency for self-sabotage. We align the circumstances in our lives to match our own expectations about what we deserve. When we live our lives convinced that we are undeserving of love, that we are worth less than the people around us, we will often set up the conditions in our world to make those beliefs a reality. In many ways, it is more important for people to be consistent than happy. We create self-fulfilling prophesies to prove ourselves right.

We find a start on the path to healing when we recognize our pain and are brave enough to let it evolve and pass. Many of us hold onto our hurt without ever realizing how much we contribute to the perpetuation of the damage. There is nothing wrong with appreciating the severity of being in a horrific situation. It is in this acknowledgement that we take the vital step towards acceptance.

By accepting the reality of the situation, without feeling obligated to justify or endorse its negatives aspects, we can find a renewed sense of purpose and of meaning. Radical acceptance is simply resigning ourselves to the fact that things happened as they did, free of judgment, and that they could not have happened any differently. It's the first step to letting go of anger and forgiving the people involved without waiting for permission or external validation. By accepting things as they are and choosing to move on, we salvage our lives, not in the frame of victims, but as survivors.

Likewise, it is important to acknowledge that the suicidal thoughts and feelings being experienced are valid. When a person feels confined and over-powered by a horrific set of circumstances, it is perfectly normal to think about suicide. This does not qualify someone as defective. However, there is a social tendency, which is even commonplace in many traditional therapies, to denounce these feelings as flawed. This judgment robs the person of a sense of validity in their thoughts and feelings. As a result, it can cause them to become more active in their suicide plan.

Horrible things sometimes happen that shake us to our roots. When those injuries result from the actions of those closest to us, we are often much less prepared to handle them. The tragedy of this story is that Eric chose a per-manent solution to a set of temporary problems. He was unable to see the blessing that he was given a clean slate from a relationship that was not healthy.

Rather than experiencing a rebirth, he chose to punish himself by hanging on to the hope for a life that was no longer there. He allowed his sense of self-worth to be entirely determined by the very person who caused the damage. Until the very end, he continued to approach Sarah with kindness and love, in spite of her rejections, without granting himself the same considerations.

The goal in any journey of healing is the same: to transform anguish into achievement. Survival depends on how meaningful life will be in the future, regardless of how painful the experience is along the way. It is not a per-son's suicidal impulses that are important but, rather, how he or she responds to them.

This is the danger of limited and inflexible thinking. When we have difficulty letting go and accepting change in our lives, we shut ourselves off from potentially new and exciting sets of circumstances. There is impermanence in the way of things that can sometimes force us to leave our pond and explore new waters. While it can be terrifying to reevaluate the circumstances of our lives in these moments, there are always potential benefits in what we might find elsewhere. This is why delaying the inevitable is often enough to circumvent a suicide attempt. Hope begins to restore itself when a person can imagine a life free of the problems and adverse situations that have caused, and continue to inflame, their suicidal crisis.

From this ethos has arisen a new wave of "solution-focused" therapies that are showing promising results, especially in the area of suicide recovery. In these systems, a therapist will have their clients focus on solutions to their circumstances, rather than concentrating on the tribulations that have caused their initial spiral into hopelessness. The goal is to create the conditions for minor victories by amplifying the positive ways in which the client can improve his or her current state of existence.

It takes persistence and dedication to see the changes that we want realized. For a person in the midst of a crisis, finding the perseverance to do this can be difficult. The decision to fight has to come from an internal spark before it can set the fires of change alight.

THEORIES OF SUICIDE

The reason as to why someone would ultimately choose this fate has been considered by many great minds and, subsequently, has been backed by ample scientific research. This deliberation has spanned across many fields, from psychology and psychiatry, to biology and genetics, sociology and anthropology, neuroscience, and beyond. While a thorough investigation into these theories goes beyond the scope of this chapter, a brief overview may provide some perspective into the cases being discussed.

In the stress-diathesis model of depression, it is theorized that the feelings of sadness and despair associated with depression lay dormant as a cognitive-vulnerability until they are triggered by a stressful event or situation. Despair or loss, either real or imagined, act as one such catalyst. In the case of a person who is at risk of committing suicide, traumatic loss, combined with the perception that there is no hope that things will get better in the future, may function as the stressor that results in an attempt. Stressful life events cluster in the weeks or months before the suicide, with desolation and hopelessness grounding the idea that escape is the only choice.

Theories of self-aggression and self-loathing consider masochistic tendencies and self-injury in an individual. While self-injury can act as a psychological means of gaining back a feeling of control, as is often seen in the case of "cutting", the lethality of the method used can sometimes result in death. What is meant as a cry for help results in fatal and irreversible damage to the body, consequently preventing medical intervention, as a result.

Suicide also occurs as a self-punishment to expiate guilt. When a person is no longer able deal with the internal anguish caused by a guilty conscience, they may seek release in death. This guilt may manifest from an event that is either real or imagined.

Durkheim posited three possible socio-cultural reasons for suicide. The first reason is called "The Egoistic", whereby a person seeks release from excessive social isolation. The individual feels a profound sense of separation between themselves and the group. They live in a subjective state of seclusion in the world around them. Supporting evidence for this idea is based in the fact that those who are unmarried, have no children, and who are not a part of any religious group are statistically more likely to commit suicide. The second reason is called "The Altruistic", resulting from those who have difficulty separating themselves and their beliefs from the group and involvement in group goals. Evidence for this comes from cult studies and suicide bombings. The third reason he called "The Anomic", posited to stem from a state of normlessness. An individual experiences a dramatic change and is unable to cope with it. They choose to die as a means of escape.

In rarer cases, suicide is thought to result from the belief that it will generate a rebirth or magical act. The person feels that a better life is waiting for them in a continued afterlife, as is thought to be the case for many suicide bombers. Alternatively, the person believes that by killing themselves they are actually dying for the sins of those around them, thereby killing the badness in the world and saving others, as seen in many documented schizophrenic suicides.

Physical illnesses, especially when terminal, are also considered to be risk factors for suicide. Rather than facing a life of pain, the person chooses to end their suffering before the illness progresses. Alternatively, they choose to end their life because they believe that the situation will never get better.

The last theory to consider is that of biological determiners. There is significant statistical evidence that suggests that a person is at a greater risk if there is a history of suicide in the family. Monozygotic twin studies have also yielded evidence of significant correlations in suicide rates. The question is what, exactly, is being inherited? Some evidence points to low serotonin and dopamine levels, while other studies have suggested deficiencies in certain transporter genes. To date, the exact cause of these statistical correlations is not yet known.

It's important to realize that even the brightest minds in the world rarely speak in absolutes behind closed doors. As such, any one particular explanation should be considered a likely truth existing interwoven as part of a more complex dynamic. Moreover, there is a risk at attempting to explain a suicide post-hoc, as there is always the possibility that a critical detail will get overlooked or that bias will influence the analysis. Rarely will a death fit neatly into a theorem and, as such, these should be only be considered guides to understanding.

STORY OF SUSAN

Susan was seventy-six years old and living in a nursing home. She had four children, but only one was taking the initiative to care for her. Her social support network was small, but the on-site nurses were a source of comfort. She felt lonely. The friends in her life had passed away from old age and her family members were too busy to come visit her regularly. Her sense of self-worth was tied to the circumstances and she took it as a reflection of how much she was loved.

She had a history of depression and had spent time in therapy building up coping mechanisms to deal with her issues. For many years, she lived happily without being plagued by her stormy emotional past. As the years progressed, she felt an ever-growing sense of meaninglessness in her life. Her children had grown up and she felt as if they no longer needed her. She longed for a renewed sense of purpose and meaning, but none came. These situations began to weigh heavy on her mind and caused a relapse in her depressive symptoms.

There was also cause for concern in terms of her physical health. She had a history of heart problems and her condition was deteriorating. She had recently developed ulcers and was sleeping poorly because she was in constant pain. The medications that she was taking were making her feel drowsy and she frequently complained of vertigo.

The nursing reports that we had on file described her mood as increasingly withdrawn in the months leading up to her death. Susan had stopped participating in events at the home and had become more socially isolated. Her family reported that she was less communicative and expressive with them. She had also stopped maintaining care in her appearance and her personal hygiene.

As the weeks passed, Susan had begun the process of systematically unplugging herself from her life before shutting down. Paradoxically, rather than getting more involved with others to combat her escalating sense of loneliness, she chose to remove herself from all potentially positive social situations. She was not feeling internally validated and slowly distanced herself from potential new sources of external support.

Susan spoke about her feelings of isolation to her family, and some of the on-site nurses, but never expressed any overt desire to die. Her detachment from the present was noticed by others but was dismissed as part of her depression, as a temporary state that would pass. On her last night, she drank a large quantity of sleeping pills and went to sleep. She did not leave a suicide note.

DISCUSSION

Seniors, in particular, are a statistically high-risk demographic for suicide. While older adults are less likely to make an attempt, they are significantly more likely to complete attempts when they do. They also tend to give fewer warnings to others of their suicidal plans, are less likely to endorse suicidal ideation when asked, use more violent and potentially lethal methods when they attempt, and apply those methods with greater planning and resolve. This is particularly true of older white males. Prevention after the onset of a suicidal crisis is also less likely to succeed later in life than at early ages. These facts are troubling considering that seniors are the fastest growing demographic worldwide.

In many ways, these are unprecedented times for elderly populations. Never before has there been such a divide between life at the start of the last century and today. The world as we know it has gone through drastic changes in social structures and family dynamics, as well in industrial and technological innovations. We are more culturally diversified and connected worldwide in a way that has never been before. These realities can have a significant influence on feelings of social isolation and environmental safety experienced by elderly populations.

News outlets and other forms of media also continue to perpetuate the idea that the world is a much more dangerous place than it was in the past. This propagation of fear can have a significant impact on persons who are already having difficulties adapting to a world where the rules of life have seemingly changed. A subjective perception of fear and uncertainty in the world at large can act as a risk factor, adding to the other personal pressures already experienced by the individual.

This group chooses suicide rationally and the belief that the world has changed for the worse can considerably contribute to an individual's decision to depart from it. This is particularly true in situations of cognitive rigidity where a person believes that a degrading social order and general moral backslide is a global and permanent state of affairs. Our emotions are intricately tied to our environment and our feelings of peace and happiness may be considerably affected when we do not feel as if we belong, that we are safe, and that we have a purpose.

Social pressures are not the only cause for concern, as suicide later in life is associated with disruptions in neural pathways that are critical to the regulation of mood, cognition, and behavior. Serotonergic, noradrenergic, and neuroendocrine systems also seem to be involved. These changes are thought to arise due to aging and gender-related changes in neurobiological systems. While this seems to be more pronounced in men than in women, both genders are at risk.

As for her family, they were overcome with guilt and anger by her death. They blamed the nursing home for allowing this to happen. At the same time, they blamed themselves for not taking her complaints of isolation seriously.

She was surrounded by people her own age in the home and they believed that whatever social comfort she needed would have been readily available to her. They spoke to her on the phone as often as they could but never noticed any inkling of suicidal thoughts. They knew that she felt abandoned. They did not know that she exacerbated this condition with her self-imposed social isolation.

While it may seem that our pain, both physical and emotional, is a permanent state of affairs, it is that exact pain that is a part of us that is asking for attention and understanding. While people are generally good at self-regulating moderate levels of pain and discomfort, there is still a tendency to get swept up in the hurt and prevalent emotions without stopping to ask ourselves what our bodies and minds really need for healing. In a very natural way, suffering is inevitable and it takes courage to want to work with it.

We have the capacity to see these things within us and achieve massive amounts of change in short periods of time. In the same capacity, we are also masters at avoiding the things that scare us, whether that be a life without someone whom we love, the feeling of being trapped in a situation that is beyond our control, intense loneliness, or the continuation of pain and suffering. We all experience tribulations and setbacks and how we think about them dramatically impacts how we feel. When we are left alone with our thoughts and do not seek out other perspectives during troubling times we may find ourselves at risk of falling victim to our own preconceptions and blinders. When we have convinced ourselves that there is no way out from the misery, many have chosen death rather than facing a life of perpetual suffering.

It is when the person believes the state of suffering is permanent, that there is no hope that circumstances will improve, that coping mechanisms can become overwhelmed. In this way, suicide is a method to be free of this suffering, the self, and these undesirable circumstances. But, regardless of age, there is always a way of changing our environment, our social circumstances, and our own internal conditions for the better.

Susan left very little in ways of a personal explanation of her decision. Her choice and reasons were her own. In some ways, it seemed as if it was a means of gaining back a sense of control. In all the ways that decisions were being made in her life on her behalf, this was one way of controlling her own destiny.

HISTORICAL HIGHLIGHTS ON SUICIDE

It is interesting to consider how modern day conceptions of suicide have changed over time. In many ways, the current discourse on the subject is a wink to ideologies of ancient cultures and thinkers. Our current social beliefs have traceable roots tracing back to the Classical philosophers, as well as to the religious thinkers of the Medieval Ages. To quote the old adage: In order to know where are going, we need to know where we have been.

In Ancient Greece and Rome, a citizen had the right to petition the senate for the right to die. In most city-states, self-killing was illegal. However, suicide was considered acceptable and, even rational, in some cases. For instance, when a person suffered from a mental illness, when the suicide was performed as per a judicial order, when it was the result of severe and unavoidable hardships, or when it was the product of extreme shame. Social roles and obligations were strongly considered in the deliberation. For this reason, slaves and soldiers were denied the right to petition, as they were considered someone else's property.

Classical philosophers had varying opinions on the subject. Plato and Aristotle considered suicide as an act of moral disrepute. Cicero believed that suicide is defensible when a person's circumstances are filled with contradictions that are not in accordance with nature. With Cicero, we begin to see an evolution in thought, as he moves beyond strictly discussing our obligations to others to include the state of the individual's well being.

For Seneca, he took this notion one step further by claiming that it is the quality of a person's life that matters, rather than the quantity. A wise person will live as long as they ought and not for as long as they can. The Stoics believed that the act is justified when the means to living a fruitful and fulfilled life were unobtainable. They did not call into question the moral character of the individual.

With the advent of Christianity, the social climate regarding suicide changed dramatically. Life was now considered to be a sacred gift from God and there was a wide-reaching religious ban against the act. Suicide corpses were desecrated, funeral services were denied, and the bodies of the victims were buried separately from others. The state would also confiscate the property of the individual.

In the literary world, we also saw a dramatic shift during this period. St. Augustine and St. Thomas Aquinas both condemned the act as an unrepentable sin. They believe that the act was against the tenets of self-love, injured the community as a whole, and violated our duties to God. Christian philosophers continued this outright rejection of suicide late into the seventeenth century. Even liberal philosophers, such as John Locke, continued to denounce the right to die.

Things started to change again in the eighteenth century as Thomistic natural law came increasingly under attack. David Hume formally challenged Thomas Aquinas in his 1783 essay "Of Suicide". He refuted his belief by rejecting the notion of 'divine order' as prohibiting the act, of social reciprocity taking precedence over our own personal responsibilities towards the self, and of suicide violating the tenets of self-love.

However, this was not true of all thinkers during this period. The most notable advocate against suicide was Immanuel Kant. For Kant, our rational wills were the root of our moral obligations and stood as a contradiction that the same will should have the right to destroy itself. This type of desecration would stand as a debasement of the very humanity within the individual.

Throughout the late eighteenth and nineteenth century, there was a continued progression regarding the treatment of the subject. With the recognition of psychology as an independent field, works began to emerge that contemplated the underlying conditions that could lead to suicide. In other literary areas, writers such a Rousseau and Goethe discussed the concept of suicide as a natural response for a tormented soul that has been rejected by love or society. Sociologists, such as Durkheim, contemplated suicide as a product of modernity and widespread alienation.

Twentieth century existentialists, such as Camus and Sartre, considered suicide as the abandonment of our responsibility in facing the absurdity of existence. They considered the act as a temptation towards an illusory promise of freedom. This was not principally based from moral concerns but rather from the consideration of man as the sole source of meaning in an otherwise meaningless universe.

In hindsight, it is clearer how the debate has opened back up in a meaningful way. Individual rights have taken center stage again in discussions regarding euthanasia and the right to die, the extent of governmental role in regulating suicide, and our privilege to choose our own state of existence. At the same time, religious philosophies remain ubiquitous in our legal and political systems. Where the debate will end up is hard to predict but it is likely going to reflect back to cyclical nature of history.

THE STORY OF ROBERT

Robert was a successful businessman with a wife and three children. He was in his mid-fifties, had a large social support network, and had no previously diagnosed cases of mental illness in his medical history. His friends and family described him as a kind-hearted and thoughtful person, but the extents of these qualities were not fully appreciated until after he had already killed himself.

What makes Robert a special case is that he took well over a year of planning before he successfully followed through with his decision. Every member of his family was considered, as were his close friends, and the people with whom he worked. He spent his time making sure that all loose ends were tied-up and that each person he cared about would be taken care of when he was gone.

He left behind a neatly typed package divided into categories for each person in his life. There was a personalized note for each person within, often several pages in length, explaining his decision and what he had done to make things more comfortable for them. His office work was completed three months in advance so that they would have time to interview his replacement. He made sure that all the financials for his family were taken care of for several years to come. Everybody was left with a goodbye, a reminder of how much he loved them, and just how much they meant to him.

Suicide notes rarely describe a complete picture. Robert was a true exception in this way. His suicide package read as a synthetical thesis discussing the details of his existential turmoil, as well as providing new insights into the way that the world works and how we relate to one another. He discussed his moral struggle with his decision and how he came to his eventual resolution. His feelings of general disconnection were explored at length. Likewise, the wearing down of his coping abilities was described in detail.

As he explained it, suicide was a strong desire of his since he was eleven years old. Although he came from a loving household, and had good friends at school, he always felt like he was living his life from the outside looking in. He never felt like he belonged or that he connected to this world in any meaningful way. Years later, this feeling festered in his marriage and family life. A sense of detachment from his life developed and a feeling of dissatisfaction grew with it.

He made a previous attempt when he was sixteen years old by slitting his wrists. Later that night, he woke up to find himself stabilized in the emergency ward of the hospital. At the time, the doctor discussed with him possibility and usefulness of hospitalization. He was committed for two months before being allowed back home.

This time, he made a plan with care, setting up the conditions for his death in the exact manner of his choosing. He hid his tracks diligently and never discussed it with his friends or family. He lived his life normally, spent time with his relatives and friends, and patiently waited for everything to be in place.

On his final day, he went to work, as usual. He came home that night, went to the basement, left the package in a visible place, and hung himself. He was discovered later that night when his family came home.

DISCUSSION

Oftentimes, delaying the inevitable may be enough to have the person rethink their position. However, Robert took his time and kept this decision to himself. There was no indication of warning and, while we'd like to believe that anyone looking to kill themselves must be certifiably insane, it would seem that he reached this decision from a place of calm introspection.

We did not code for any prevalent mental illness post-hoc. This was surprising as the vast majority of completers have at least one diagnosable mental disorder. We also know that most will meet criteria for clinical depression. However, neither friends, nor family, were able to help us uncover one that could have helped to explain what happened.

Robert had a strong social support network, was financially secure, had no recorded history of mental illness, no familial history of suicide, and even appeared to be happy until his dying day. The choice was made independently and without coercion from external influences. He was not drunk or under the influence of any drugs at the time at the death. In fact, it appeared throughout the investigation as if he was in a sound mental state throughout the process.

All indications pointed to a long-standing existential crisis as the root cause of his chosen escape. He was overwhelmed by the enormity of his problem and saw suicide as a logical way out. He wrote that death was a welcome release and that he embraced it with open arms.

Robert's family expressed remorse at the fact that they never knew his subjective state of mind until it was too late. He felt alone and disconnected even when he was surrounded in the people who loved him the most. His wife knew about his previous suicide attempt but thought that it was a callous act of an impulsive adolescent. She thought that period in his life was long over and could not understand how he could have planned for so long without telling her how he felt.

He lived his life with the ongoing and continual consideration of suicide. As he described it, it was always in the back of his mind as a way out. Even with his explanations, it is difficult to say exactly what sparked his decision to die. Perhaps it was his pervasive contemplation on the subject led to the calm and methodical decision that he did not want to live anymore. His family and friends were considered at length but even they were not enough of a reason to dissuade him from his choice.

His decision was not the result of an isolated and temporary set of circumstances. His reasons were not environmental or social in nature. Rather, his dissatisfaction came from an internal feeling of social segregation and exclusion. While others willingly accepted him in their lives, he never felt like he was one of them.

The systematized preparation for his death took precedence over everything else. Every day was another step closer to his follow through. He lived his life with ample opportunity to change his mind. Yet, nothing deterred him in all the time that he patiently waited.

The idea that someone would want to end their life by a rational and calm choice can be extremely threatening to our own egos and sense of mortality and self-preservation. In this writer's personal opinion, adults of sound mental faculty, fully aware of their situation and the potential consequences of their actions, should have the right to make their own choice regarding their state of existence. To believe otherwise is a slippery slope whereby the infringement of individual human rights and freedoms may result.

Nevertheless, it is important to bear in mind the ways in which we can rediscover a sense of personal meaning in our existence. Robert's existential crisis was always concentrated on his feelings of belonging. Viktor Frankl, the father of Logotherapy, believed that as a person rediscovers a sense of personal meaning in life, their noogenic neurosis would heal and their existential vacuum would be filled. Robert may have been able to find a renewed sense of purpose and connection with others by striving for higher ideals and reshaping his goals. Potentially, he might have started to see his situation in a completely different way.

More to the point, if an adult is determined to end his or her life, there is little anyone can do to stop it in the long-term. While it may sound inhumane, as if the very suggestion is a silent endorsement of the option, I suggest it free of judgment. I simply accept it as simply the way of things, much like many others that are beyond our control.

POST-THOUGHTS

One of the paradoxes of suicide is that it can seem as if it happens as the result of a single reason. The decision to die is not a random decision but the result of a build-up. There is an ever present cycle of tormenting thoughts that the person experiences day after day. When a person is living in this spiraling state of mind they experience a wearing away of their mental resistance. Risk factors begin to pile up and stressors remain prevalent and unyielding in the individual's perception of events. Somewhere along this spectrum, a moment occurs when the threshold limit of tolerance is reached and the scales may tip in favor of death.

However, just because a person is having difficulty in one area of their life now, doesn't mean they are incompetent in other areas of their life. Current problems do not indicate future or past issues. Minor positive changes act as catalysts to recovery. These victories can start to outweigh problem circumstances as practical small steps lead to achievements. Achievements bolster self-esteem, resulting in a restored feeling of competence and self-worth. It is in seeing potential for long-term change that we feel a renewed sense of vitality towards our efforts. After a few minor victories, a steadfast resolve often develops where the person is not willing to settle for anything less than the total attainment of their goals. This improved state of self is vital to tipping the scales back in favor of life.

The ways in which we choose to see life has a powerful impact on our feelings of belonging and connection to the world. Our feelings of existential peace, happiness, and meaning are intricately tied to our environment, social world, and subjective internal states. Furthermore, how we choose to see death will shape how we decide to leave this world. It can be a beautiful departure or a horrific escape.

Suicide is a choice but one that rarely comes as the result of a calm and introspective decision; rather, it is likely a reaction to a set of circumstances. Death is a final solution when a person believes that there is no other option. As a practical consideration, there is more potential to life than we could ever hope to realize. It should logically go that all other alternatives should be explored first. Oftentimes, many of these options remain unexplored before it is too late.

Prediction is difficult, as risk factors can apply to anyone, but we can take solace in the fact that suicide is a rare event. Some of you may have known someone who is the victim of suicide. Some of you may even know someone who is currently calling out for help. I hope that somewhere in the preceding pages you found clarity to some of your questions or even just the realization that you are not alone.

MISCARRIAGE, ABORTION, AND INFERTILITY

The Invisible Death

© 2012 barbara cameron pix

THE INVISIBLE PRESSURE OF BEING A WOMAN CAN CAUSE
IMMEASUREABLE GRIEF IF YOU DON'T BEAR A CHILD

I have been thinking about the death of unborn loves and was moved to explore this unique loss that women experience viscerally. I realized almost immediately how uniquely private the relationship is between a women and her yet to be born child. I then began to understand how intimate the death of the unborn child must be. As I looked further into this gender-specific loss, I sensed a need to make this type of 'private' death more understood and honored by all of us.

I see three distinct deaths of a yet-to-be-born loved one; abortion, miscarriage, and infertility. The first two are a death of an unborn yet physical body. The third is the loss of the dream, the urge, the bodily desire of birthing a child. Here are some statistics I discovered as I was doing research for this piece:

In Canada in 2004 there were 337,072 births, 96,815 abortions and 55,280 miscarriages. These numbers surprised me. I had no idea about this rather private world of women and their unborn deaths. Of course I know about miscarriage and abortion; it was the magnitude of the numbers that shocked me. Two hundred and sixty four abortions each day in Canada, one hundred and fifty one miscarriages each day seemed significant to me.

I am not making a judgment here. I am recognizing that no matter what the cause of unborn death is, they are in fact a death and a loss to the woman and those close to her. It is another type of death wrapped in silence and taboo.

The unborn baby was created in the body of the woman and also died inside her—a very private affair. This invisible, unseen birth and death brings with it a different set of grief and bereavement issues particularly for the mothers. The woman is dealing with not only the physical effects of conception but also the grief of the loss of her unborn child.

A second unique issue is the lack of a body, a funeral, a lack of closure. In the case of a death of a loved one we have lots of structure and processes to mark life and death. Most often with a miscarriage there is not a noticeable body nor is there a formal funeral or ceremony. As a result people are uncertain how to respond and what to say. Often they choose to stay silent and the woman who has suffered the loss of her child is bound to grieve alone or perhaps with her partner.

Here is a list of unique losses that are common to miscarriage:
- The loss of the opportunity to be a mother
- The loss of trust in her body
- The loss of a full and joyous pregnancy
- The loss of the unborn child

There are very real feelings that arise: shame, guilt and embarrassment are some of unique ones. These feeling and emotions are complicated by the fact that the woman's body is going through significant hormonal changes on top of the emotional impact of the loss.

The woman may feel she has let her partner down. She may be feeling the pain of not knowing the sex of the child, or seeing its body. The mother may be confused about why she feels so much grief about a child she has never seen.

Coupled with these issues is the lack of answers and the inability to understand why. The medical system is often unable to provide answers to the miscarriage. When they do speak to the woman it can often be in medically insensitive language that can sound like; *the pregnancy terminated*, or *the tissue was passed*. Oftentimes they may refer to the miscarriage as a minor medical occurrence.

Women can feel pressured by others and often by themselves to try to get pregnant again quickly, not taking the time to allow the grief from their miscarriage to pass. This can have consequences, such as partnership stress and/or post-natal depression. Women are always looking for answers to 'why' and, although there must be reasons, they do not usually find out what they are. So miscarriage grief is not so much about finding the answer they yearn for, as learning how to live without one.

There are also no pictures and few memories that we can hold dear as we remember the unborn loved one. Unlike other deaths, the woman's relationship with her child was 'internal' and very short. Others may not understand the depth of love that the mother had for her child and minimize the loss.

Then there is the long list of 'what ifs' many women go through. What if I had more rest and not worked so hard? What if I had eaten more nutritional food? What if I were in better physical safe before I got pregnant?

In the case of abortion, although there is a degree of choice involved, women may still suffer grief. Similar to miscarriage, it is difficult to talk about, especially given it was a considered choice. Women may be afraid to talk about it, may feel great shame about their abortion, and may not even realize how it is affecting them. Many women are often afraid to talk about their abortion to their doctor or counselor and certainly do not wish it to become public possibly facing harsh criticism. Some women state that they are "okay" or that "it was the best decision they could have made for that time in their life." All this outward behavior may be masking a deep sense of grief.

Women struggling with abortion-related grief may experience some or all of these symptoms or upsets:

- A general sense of depression and anxiety
- A numbing of emotions and feelings
- A non-specific feeling of loss
- Anger and resentment
- Sudden and unexplained periods of crying
- A change in relationship with partner
- A lack of desire to be intimate and sexual
- A loss of sleep and inability to sleep
- Addictive tendencies for food, alcohol, or drugs

Be aware of the signals, pay attention to them, and ask for support from a therapist or hospice worker if you are experiencing any of them. The clinic will be a resource for you if you recognize any.

In the case of infertility it is challenging for others to really understand the grief a woman may be going through. Procreation is a basic and primal function common in human beings. It is normal to have strong feelings about sex, pregnancy, and birth. Many women have an innate mothering instinct that sometimes can be beyond reason and control. It is a natural part of living and no shame or embarrassment should be attached to how we feel about the loss of a baby at whatever stage. Even the thought and planning to having a child is like a birth of sorts.

For women who are infertile, have tried to conceive, even utilizing expensive, lengthy and troublesome fertility process and are still unable to conceive the grief can be deep and consuming. There is mistaken shame and a sense of not truly being a woman. Many of the signs and symptoms of grief explained above apply here. Others, friends and family, may have a difficulty relating to her loss and the depth of her grief or shame. For some women, who have always desperately wanted to experience pregnancy and childbirth, the grieving process may be intense and prolonged.

Even if the woman chooses adoption the issue of infertility and its associated grief do not go away. The door is never fully closed on that grief or loss. When her adoptive child reaches childbearing age, the issue may come up again. When grandchildren are born, she may look at the child and wonder, "Who does this child look like? Certainly not me!"

No matter which of these three private and invisible deaths a woman experiences, her grief is real and needs to be expressed, received, and honored. So go ahead and talk about it. You can be proud of your pregnancies, and your attempts to have a child no matter how unfulfilled they were. A hurt heart is a sign of your capacity to love deeply! One thing that can really help women through this 'private grief' is to know other women who have been through the same thing. There is no reason for you to be alone.

CLOSING NOTES

I want to thank each of you for joining me on this real and personal journey along the path of death. I am hopeful that you found something helpful that will make future experiences with death more graceful, real and enlivening. Welcome to the new conversation.

If you feel inclined to connect with me please do so by emailing me at stephen@embraceyourdeath.com. I would love to hear from you.

Printed in Canada